T0356679

Advance Praise for *The Adult Chair*

"Michelle Chalfant has a brilliant gift for explaining deeply healing concepts and practices. One of my favorite things about Michelle Chalfant and *The Adult Chair* is how she shares her own life experiences, offering real examples of working through triggers. Her vulnerability and authenticity are a breath of fresh air, especially for those of us in the mental health and healing fields. She truly embodies the 'inner work' she teaches, making her an inspiring guide on the path to transformation."

—Liz Burkholder, PhD, mind-body medicine, holistic nurse practitioner and founder of GoWithin Institute

"With Michelle Chalfant's beautiful real-life examples, along with practical how-to lists, anyone could read this book and be set on a true path to self-transformation and healing. This is a remarkable achievement!"

—Dr. Pam Staples, founder of Relational Joy

"*The Adult Chair* distills complex ideas into accessible insights and practical tools. Whether you're on a journey of self-discovery or striving to become your healthiest, best self, this is the road map you need to embrace life fully and fearlessly."

—Amberly Lago, *USA Today* bestselling author of *Joy Through the Journey*

"In the ten years I have known Michelle Chalfant, I have never ceased to be amazed by her unique ability to merge kindness, empathy, intellect, and a profound, almost otherworldly sense of understanding of grief and trauma. *The Adult Chair* is a testament to these qualities, offering readers a transformative approach to emotional healing."

—Ross Rosenberg, M.Ed., LCPC, CADC, author of *The Human Magnet Syndrome* and *The Codependency Revolution*

"*The Adult Chair* offers a powerful, interactive journey out of the often-murky depths of childhood wounds into lasting transformation. Keep pen and paper handy—you'll want to engage deeply with each thoughtfully crafted exercise designed to support profound growth and sustainable change."

—PATTI ELLEDGE, Somatic Experiencing practitioner and mentor; adult attachment specialist

"Michelle Chalfant's openness and honesty in sharing how she has applied the Adult Chair Model to her own life—leading to profound and sustainable change—will make readers feel like they truly have a coach in their corner whom they can trust. This book is a beautiful gift that we can all benefit from."

—KAREN GELSTEIN, Trauma and Addiction Therapist; EMDR and somatic practitioner

"If you are ready to get unstuck, truly understand yourself on the deepest level, and break past old limiting patterns or cycles that are holding you back, no matter how long they may have been repeating in your life, this is a must-read."

—ELYSE ARCHER, founder and CEO, She Sells

"*The Adult Chair* is both deeply illuminating and incredibly actionable. This book is a game changer."

—PREMA GAIA, founder of Nervous System Support

"A powerful guide for anyone seeking deeper self-awareness and emotional freedom. Michelle Chalfant offers a clear and compassionate framework that helps us navigate life with greater balance, confidence, and authenticity. *The Adult Chair* is an invaluable resource for those ready to step into their fullest potential."

—CATHERINE PLANO, PhD, MCC, founder of Rise & Thrive Global and author of *Shifts Only Happen Once You Own Your Sh!t*

"Michelle Chalfant has created a life-changing guide, brilliantly illuminating how we lose ourselves along the way and, more importantly, how we can reclaim our power, confidence, and authenticity in our adult lives."

—JESSICA PAPINEAU, CEO and founder of CSJ Authentic Fashion Styling

The
Adult Chair

Get Unstuck, Claim Your Power,
and Transform Your Life

Michelle Chalfant

CONVERGENT

NEW YORK

Convergent
An imprint of Random House
A division of Penguin Random House LLC
1745 Broadway, New York, NY 10019
convergentbooks.com
penguinrandomhouse.com

LIBRARY OF CONGRESS CATALOGING-IN-PUBLICATION DATA
Names: Chalfant, Michelle, author.
Title: The adult chair / by Michelle Chalfant.
Description: First edition. | New York: Convergent Books, an imprint of
Random House, a division of Penguin Random House LLC, [2025] |
Includes bibliographical references.
Identifiers: LCCN 2024054045 (print) | LCCN 2024054046 (ebook) |
ISBN 9780593735336 (hardcover) | ISBN 9780593735343 (ebook)
Subjects: LCSH: Psychotherapy—Popular works. | Psychotherapy—
Anecdotes. | Mental health—Popular works.
Classification: LCC RC480.515 .C43 2025 (print) | LCC RC480.515
(ebook) | DDC 616.89/14—dc23/eng/20250208
LC record available at https://lccn.loc.gov/2024054045
LC ebook record available at https://lccn.loc.gov/2024054046

Printed in the United States of America on acid-free paper

2   4   6   8   9   7   5   3   1

First Edition

The authorized representative in the EU for product safety and compliance is
Penguin Random House Ireland, Morrison Chambers, 32 Nassau Street,
Dublin D02 YH68, Ireland. https://eu-contact.penguin.ie

To my family, both past and present.
For the love that surrounded me,
the traumas that challenged me,
and every experience in between.
Each moment has shaped me into the person I am today.
I am eternally grateful.

Contents

The Adult Chair Model

A s Sara sat down for her first session, I asked, "What would you like to work on today?" She said, "I don't feel emotions. In fact, I feel quite numb inside. I get reactive with people, and it is hurting my relationships. I have worked with so many therapists and coaches, and yet I don't seem to be able to move forward. Do you think you can help me?"

Sara's story isn't unique. So many of us are living with stress, anxiety, or depression and can't seem to find relief. Others are struggling with addiction, dysfunctional relationships, or low self-worth. Maybe you've done years of therapy and still seem to be falling into the same patterns over and over. Through decades of working with countless clients, I've found that most forms of therapy, while well-meaning, focus on diagnosing and treating symptoms rather than healing the root causes.

That's why I developed the Adult Chair model. Healing is possible and happens faster with a simplified and clear understanding of who we are, how we got this way, and how to move forward. The Adult Chair model is where simple psychology meets grounded spirituality, an integrated blend of insights to help people raise their awareness and their consciousness and create powerful change in their lives.

As I explained the pillars of it to Sara, I could see a light bulb going on. She saw she had the power to change. And with change could come a more beautiful, peaceful, and authentic life.

I leaned in. "I'm glad you're here," I told Sara. "And I think this model can help you."

The Adult Chair Model and Why It Will Help

The Adult Chair model teaches people who they are and how they developed into the adults they are today. It's a comprehensive yet simple-to-understand guide that describes how the experiences of our lives have shaped us using the visual of three chairs—the Child Chair, the Adolescent Chair, and the Adult Chair—and explains why we show up the way we do in the world. It gives you the "how to" and lays out the tools to transform common issues we all face, like low self-worth, unhealthy relationships, lack of boundaries, anxiety, codependency, and more. Lastly, it illustrates what an emotionally healthy person looks like and gives us a role model to strive for using five pillars that we can put into practice daily.

Knowing these skills has transformed my life, and I want to share this with the world. It's the information that I wish I'd had in my teens and twenties when I was living with depression, anxiety, people-pleasing, and codependency. When I was going through my initial healing journey, I knew I was unhappy, in pain, and wanted help, but I couldn't find the "how to." I have walked this path of transformation and found that the Adult Chair is what I needed and longed for.

My hope is that this book provides this for you—an "owner's manual" for adults, not only outlining how to identify where things might have gone wrong in your development, but also providing tools that will teach you how to make true, lasting changes that lead to the empowered, fulfilling life you are longing for.

How can this model help you? I have seen so many examples of people finally able to get unstuck, find clarity in their lives, and feel more empowered. The model helps this process by breaking down our lives from childhood through adulthood and allowing us to see our missing milestones or where things might have gone wrong.

We learn how to be healthy functioning adults from the people who raise us. Both consciously and unconsciously, they set an example for how we show up in the world in relationship to ourselves and how much worth we have. They model for us how to cultivate and be present in our relationships of all kinds, and if we are allowed to have needs and express them or if we must stay quiet and allow others to walk all over us and treat us poorly.

Our parents demonstrate for us how to care for and love ourselves. They share their beliefs with us around health, money, and how we should be treated in the world. They teach us about God, faith, and the promise that when we die, we go to heaven (or hell). Our parents play a huge role in framing who we are and how we develop during our lives.

While growing up, we look to them as if they are gods themselves. We don't know any better. From the earliest age, we need them to feed and nurture us, and we instinctively know that they are the people we need to please and get love from—because who else will take care of us and keep us fed and safe in the world? Unconsciously we absorb all of their beliefs around how the world works, and from there learn how we should be showing up in the world.

The problem is that if we are raised in a broken home, or a dysfunctional family, or by neglectful or unhealthy parents, we learn only what they have to offer and grow into adults who are programmed with limiting beliefs about ourselves, others, and the world.

Unfortunately, we don't know what we are missing. We all do the best we can (including our parents). We do our best to function as healthy adults, but if we missed specific lessons or milestones, and don't even know what those are, it's like driving our car with a tire that needs air or is even flat.

The Adult Chair model takes you through the timeline from birth to where you are today in adulthood and helps you to understand where you might have missed an important developmental milestone or lesson.

The model also shows you how you might be compensating for this in your life now, whether through people-pleasing, numbing out, being critical of self, or any of the other unproductive coping strategies we develop (strategies that cause suffering in our lives!).

For example, you might be someone who never learned how to set clear boundaries with others, and instead learned from your parents "don't rock the boat, just give in"—to not be confrontational but to let people walk all over you. If this sounds like you, how is your life now? How are your relationships? Do you feel drained or fatigued?

Perhaps you are living with an autoimmune disease. I've seen many people in my practice who have lived with the symptoms of this type of disease and the common theme is that they did not embody a strong sense of self or set clear boundaries. They were walked on and did not speak up for themselves.

This book will help you to see things like this in your own life. When you can identify these missed lessons and then understand how they are affecting your current life, the light bulbs start coming on. Life starts to make sense. We have a raised awareness of how we are not showing up in a healthy way today and what we would like instead.

We begin to realize there is another way, and the Adult Chair model provides the road map for how to shift the areas of our lives where we feel stuck and begin to create an updated or new road map for our futures. You will begin to feel aligned with your true self, your soul self, and your whole world will begin to change.

The Three Chairs Explained

As Sara's session continued, I stood up and pulled three chairs into the center of the room. "I'm going to show you the three main developmental stages that humans go through.

By the end, I believe you will not only understand your concerns but also have a plan for how to connect with your true self and learn to feel your emotions, as well as a framework for how to create healthy relationships. Sound good?"

I could see the relief flash across her face as I began to explain to Sara the story of her life and how she got this way. Though I often use physical chairs as an experiential tool with clients, you don't need to use physical chairs to apply the Adult Chair model to your life. The chairs are ultimately a metaphor for the place we are approaching life from—the perspective we are "sitting" in.

Humans all go through the same developmental stages in life. The model illustrates these developmental phases using chairs: the Child Chair, the Adolescent Chair, and the Adult Chair. Our daily goal is to spend as much time as possible in our Adult Chair—our healthiest self. Unfortunately, unless we received perfect, healthy parenting (and none of us did), we might physically develop into adults but mentally and emotionally show up and react from our childhood wounds and from the survival mechanisms we developed in our adolescent years, or earlier.

It's important to reflect back on your formative years. By understanding the messages you received growing up and the behaviors you saw modeled, and by learning about the road map that was created during the first six years of your life, you can change and update your programming and patterns . . . and transform your life! Anyone can do this. We first need to raise our awareness of how we developed into who we are today. And that's where the three chairs come in.

The first chair, the Child Chair, represents the earliest phase of our life. This chair includes the developmental milestones that happen (or don't happen) from birth to six years of age.

During this phase, we learn many things, but most importantly we experience and learn about trust, safety, emotions, and our needs. We rely on our parents to keep us protected and safe and to take care of our needs. We may need consolation, a hug, or to hear "I love you" or "You matter so much to me." We depend heavily on our parents to witness and reflect who we are, versus projecting onto us who they want us to be.

As I explained this to Sara, she looked at me wide-eyed. "Growing up, I was shamed for crying and speaking up," she said. She shared that her mom had had three children under six years old, and she was completely overwhelmed all the time. Her mom couldn't handle the kids' emotions or needs and would fly into a rage when any of the kids would cry. I could see Sara was starting to put the pieces together, but we next needed to uncover what had developed during her adolescent years.

The Adolescent Chair is the next developmental stage. It's a larger age range—from age seven to twenty-four—and a lot happens during these years.

During this phase of development, we leave the feeling of oneness and connectedness that children experience and begin to see ourselves as separate individuals. This is due to the development of our ego. It causes us to develop a sense of individual identity, and we begin to see ourselves as an "I" instead of a "we."

It's important to note that this is a completely normal and necessary step of our development and human experience. To grow from childhood to adulthood is to learn how to take care of ourselves and function independently of our family unit in the world. However, this development also makes us begin to feel separate from our mother, family, and the oneness/Source/God energy that we came from and are part of, and with this separation comes fear that we are alone. And with fear comes a number of coping mechanisms and survival strategies to keep us safe, connected, and feeling like we belong.

While in this chair, because of our ego, we leave the present moment and instead live in the past and future, making up stories and assumptions to keep ourselves safe.

Our ego ideas are based on subconscious programming and limiting thoughts, which can result in reactivity and defensiveness.

We react without facts, and we are quick to judge self or others. Disconnected from the true needs and emotions of our Child Chair, we instead learn how to numb our pain and reach for things outside of us to feel okay—especially if our parents didn't model how to handle our emotions in a healthy way. This can lead us to adopt compulsions and addictions to things that, in the moment, make us feel better, such as social media, Netflix, porn, drugs, alcohol, food, shopping, drama, or even chaos.

One of our Adolescent's strategies is to create masks that it thinks will keep us safe. This is where the inner critic, fraud, judger, helper, perfectionist, people pleaser, and more begin to show up in our lives. As they do, we unconsciously cover up who we truly are and build a false self that overlays, *masks,* our true self. We fall asleep to our true selves and forget who we really are.

So many of the common challenges we face, so many of the things that keep us stuck, can be traced back to this stage of development.

As Sara reflected back on her adolescent self, she began to see how she had started blocking her emotions so as not to provoke her mother's anger. I explained this could be where the irritation to emotions was coming from. Her Adolescent simply didn't know what to do with them.

And the outcome of this was showing itself in her relationships, where she was short-tempered and hurting people. She needed her Adult! She was physically an adult but living from her Adolescent.

It bears repeating that the stage itself is not "bad," but the danger is that most of us carry the unhealthy strategies we learned here into adulthood. They become like an operating manual or road map that we build our lives from, even when they no longer serve us and who we are now.

Only by learning how to mature into a healthy adult and manage these parts of ourselves can we find peace, freedom, and a restored connection with our true selves.

And that's where the Adult Chair comes in, which is the third chair. We move into this phase around the age of twenty-five. This stage is marked by raised consciousness, awareness of self and others, and living in the present moment.

In our Adult Chair, we live with facts and truth versus stories and assumptions from our past or future. We can connect to and feel our emotions and take care of ourselves by sharing our wants and needs with others and setting boundaries.

In this stage, we live with raised awareness about our own actions, choices, and motivations. For example, if we realize we are drinking too much in the evenings, we reflect upon this and decide to stop or decrease our drinking. If we hurt someone, we own it and apologize. We work to forgive ourselves and others when needed, and not hold ourselves back from moving forward in life. We strive to live with peace and balance. And if we are not living there—and none of us do all the time—we use one of the tools in the model to get ourselves back. This is how healthy adults live.

Moving into your Adult Chair can happen quite naturally if you had modeling from parents who were emotionally healthy and helped you hit all of your developmental milestones. Unfortunately, most of us didn't get this. Most of us were raised by parents who did their best with what they knew, including what they saw modeled from their own parents. Sara saw this, as her overwhelmed mother didn't know how to channel her emotions in a healthy way and instead exploded in anger toward her children. If our parents didn't learn and experience healthy concepts like feeling and expressing their emotions, managing their triggers, setting boundaries, and cultivating self-love, how in the world are we supposed to know these things?

The result is that we physically continue to grow and mature into adults, but emotionally, we are living and making choices and decisions from our Adolescent Chair.

The good news is that regardless of what you learned or didn't learn, with curiosity, desire, and effort, you can move more and more into your Adult Chair now.

The Benefits of Living in Your Adult Chair

After I explained the chairs to Sara, she looked at me and said, "I get it! This makes so much sense! Since we didn't 'do' emotions in our home growing up, I don't know how to feel mine. No one modeled healthy emotions or sat with me when I was feeling my emotions."

"Exactly," I replied. "And because you missed out on exploring and feeling your emotions during your time in your Child Chair, our work will be to help you reconnect with your younger self and get those emotions 'activated' and flowing through your body again."

We also needed to bring in Sara's adult-self energy to help her feel and process emotions, show up in a healthy way with boundaries to get her needs met, and also learn how to apologize to anyone she has hurt. I would soon introduce her to the five pillars (more on that later), which would give her tools to put this into practice.

This was all new for her. And I could see the relief in the tears that were forming in her eyes as she thanked me. By living in the Adult Chair, you begin to uncover who you really are—your true self. This is the self you were born with. It's your true essence that is connected to something much bigger than you. Call it God, Source, Universe . . . *that* is the you that you came to this planet as, that you can still connect to and live from today.

The Work Ahead of Us

Most people start to feel better about themselves as soon as they learn about the Adult Chair model. My hope is that when you decide to take the journey of finding and living from your Adult Chair, you will have the same empowering experience as Sara and countless clients.

I've written this book to be your guide as you learn how to apply the model to your life, and it's organized into two parts.

Part 1, "The Three Chairs," will explain the three chairs and each developmental stage in detail, each chapter unpacking one of the chairs. Together, we will ask questions and reflect on your formative experiences in your childhood and adolescence, ultimately uncovering the road map that you have unconsciously been using to direct your life.

You will find some areas that you may recognize and some that you need to look at a little deeper. Take your time in this part. Breathe, take breaks, move your body—doing this work can be uncomfortable at times, but by bringing everything out into the open, the healing can finally begin.

In part 2, "The Five Pillars," you will learn the five pillars that are the hallmark of a healthy adult. These are practices that you will return to daily as you strive to live out of your Adult Chair. These pillars are:

1. I Own My Reality
2. I Practice Self-Compassion
3. I Feel My Emotions
4. I Own My Triggers
5. I Set Healthy Boundaries

In this section, I will explain these concepts as well as powerful tools and processes to put them into practice, which are simple to understand but absolutely transformational. Once they are incorporated into your life, you will find your life beginning to change, and you will start to see a new you— the you that you were born with. It is true freedom to live from your Adult Chair. It's a place of ease, balance, fun, and peace.

I look forward to walking this path alongside you. Know that I am cheering you on as we go!

PART 1

The Three Chairs

CHAPTER ONE

The Child Chair

———————⌒————————

Mary Ann came into my office asking for help with her anxiety. "I live with a lot of fear," she told me, explaining how scared she was of being trapped, which affected her when getting on airplanes. She also feared her kids were going to get in car accidents, and she found herself constantly worrying about her oldest child, who was away at college.

When she told me she'd felt like this for as long as she could remember, I knew we needed to start with the beginning of her story. "When you think back to your childhood, what stands out about the first six years of your life?" I asked.

Mary Ann thought for a moment, then responded that the biggest thing was the lack of stability at home. Her parents fought all the time, and her mother would scream at her father and threaten to leave and never come back. "I remember hiding with my little sister in her bedroom closet when they would fight. We'd be so scared of Mom leaving and not coming back."

I asked how sharing this made her feel. She looked at me

through tears and said, "I can't breathe. My whole body is tight."

"Mary Ann, how old do you feel right now?"

She immediately responded, "Four."

I knew immediately that Mary Ann's current anxiety and feelings of fear were coming from her earlier childhood programming, or her road map that was formed between the ages of zero to six years old, the time period I call the Child Chair. By starting here, with the Child Chair, Mary Ann was able to understand the story of her life: who she is and how she got this way.

So, let's begin here, with the Child Chair. First, I'll walk you through understanding how we are shaped by our parents and our childhood experiences. Then we'll take a look at how these formative experiences shape us when it comes to emotions, identifying our needs, healthy attachment, vulnerability, intimacy, passion, creativity, play, and fun. These are the parts of our road map that are meant to be formed during this stage of development. If you did not get what you needed in any of these areas during this stage of life, you will likely find you struggle in them as an adult.

Next, we'll take a look at the common ways we might be wounded as a child and how this can impact the rest of our lives. Finally, I'll teach you how to reconnect with your inner child so that you can learn from them, check in with them and identify their needs, and re-parent them in a healthier way.

I invite you to journey with me back to your younger years, open to learning and gaining new awareness about your past that will give you the understanding you need to move more solidly into your Adult Chair.

What Is the Child Chair
and Where Does It Come From?

As mentioned earlier, the Child Chair phase begins at conception and ends at around age six. A 2011 study published by the Association for Psychological Science found that "as a fetus grows, it's constantly getting messages from its mother. It's not just hearing her heartbeat and whatever music she might play to her belly; it also gets chemical signals through the placenta. This includes signals about the mother's mental state."[1]

This is incredible! As our bodies, brains, and nervous systems develop in utero, especially from the twenty-fifth week until birth, we are sensing, feeling, and absorbing what is happening in our external environments, especially that of our mother.

Think back to when your mother was pregnant with you. If you have access to this information, see if you can answer the following questions: What was the energy like in your home with your parents? Was it a stressful environment or peaceful? Were your parents fighting or were they eagerly awaiting your arrival? Did your mama sing to you and caress her belly with anticipation of your birth? Were you a planned baby or a "mistake"? Was there mental illness or addiction in the home? Was your mother afraid to bring you home? Were you given up for adoption? What might have been the conversation happening around you while you were developing? Answers to these questions can give you some important information as to what your early self was already taking in and attempting to make sense of.

At birth, we enter into the world as a pure essence of self: innocent, vulnerable, and curious about the big world we are born into. We are "blank slates"—no mental programming or wounding, no beliefs or thoughts about how the world works or who we are.

We open our eyes to a new world and are 100 percent dependent on our parents to feed, soothe, protect, nurture, and love us. They are our teachers of life, and they model for us how to act as healthy humans. Because we don't have a self-image or an understanding of who we are yet, our parents show us this by reflecting who we are, serving as mirrors for us as we build our sense of self.

Our parents have *huge* jobs. Raising a child is not easy; in fact, it can be quite overwhelming. How our parents show up for us during the first phase of development is paramount to how we develop into adults. They model and teach us the art of feeling and expressing emotions, how to speak up for ourselves and protect our personal space with boundaries, and how to be brave and confident people. They affect how we see, love, and nurture ourselves as well as others whom we develop relationships with in our future, from friends to romantic partners and even colleagues.

We are like little sponges in this phase, absorbing everything we hear, sense, and experience as 100 percent truth.

Our brains grow the fastest during these years; in fact, we develop more than one million new neural connections per second during this time.[2] This stage of development is exciting, but the issue with this super-learning phase is that as we absorb, we take in *everything* as normal and healthy—regardless of whether it actually is or not. The ability to discern good from bad and right from wrong does not fully develop until around the age of twenty-five, when the prefrontal cortex develops in our brain. That means that we store all of our childhood experiences as truth, and based on these experiences, we develop a road map for life.

The problem is that most of these beliefs, as well as our road map, live in the *unconscious* mind—"the shadow," as Carl Jung coined it. In fact, we live 95 percent from our unconscious mind and only 5 percent from our conscious mind. Most of us are unaware of the thoughts and beliefs we have (our "childhood programming"); we simply live from them.

Think about that for a moment: What you learned and experienced in the first six years of life is what you are using to navigate your life as an adult! This is how many of us live our lives—we're trying to find our way through adulthood using old information. The work of living in your Adult Chair is updating that road map with the truth you now know about your adult self.

Even though the Child Chair is developed during the first six years of life, this part is very much alive and with you. The energy of this precious part of us exists inside as what we call "the inner child."

When you are feeling emotions or tapping into your

needs, you are connecting with your inner child. When you are living with your passion and creativity, you are very much connecting to the energy of the inner child. Likewise, when you feel disconnected from your emotions, needs, passion, or creativity, this means you are blocked from your inner child. "Inner child work" is a process where you are tapping into and opening up the energy of this part of you.

Let's pause here for a moment so you can reflect on what you absorbed in your Child Chair that might now be directing your adult life. Then we'll move on to look at the key developmental milestones of this phase, so that we can identify the areas that may need to be addressed in order to move forward.

EXERCISE

Take a moment to imagine traveling back in time to when you were between the ages of zero and six, or picture yourself at that age sitting next to you. If it helps, close your eyes and take a few long, deep breaths.

1. Is there anything significant that stands out for you during these years? A death in the family, a divorce, a move, the birth of a new sibling, a sick parent, an addict in the home? What comes to your mind when you first think of this time period?

2. When you were hurt, injured, sad, or afraid, who was there to tend to you? How were you treated? Did some-

one tend to your emotions, feelings, and injuries, or were you told to get over it and move on, or even ignored?

3. Did you feel safe in your home and feel that you had someone you could go to when you needed love, support, and care? Was there yelling, fighting, bullying, or name-calling (to you or others in your home)?

4. What did fun look like in your house while growing up? Were you allowed to explore and have fun, or were you controlled or not given the opportunity to explore?

5. What did you love to do while growing up? Were you encouraged and supported, or were you ignored, belittled, or simply not supported?

Without judgment, write about these things and anything else that comes to your mind as you reflect. Remember that this is not an exercise of judgment, but instead we are looking for the facts about how you experienced your past. There is no right or wrong, just your memory of your past.

Six Key Qualities of the Child Chair

The parts of our road map that are meant to be formed during this stage of development take the forms of six key qualities: feeling our emotions; identifying our needs; expressing vulnerability; developing intimacy; nurturing passion; and engaging with creativity, play, and fun. Lastly, running through all six of these is a critically important factor that supports them all: developing a healthy attachment with our parent(s). If you did not get what you needed in any of these six areas during this stage of life, you will likely find you struggle in them as an adult.

As you read through the key qualities of the Child Chair, notice how these show up for you in your adult life. Are these qualities alive and healthy in your current life, or are they suppressed, underdeveloped, or even unknown? Consider putting a check mark next to any that you identify might need further reflection or work.

1. Emotions

As children, we experience emotions in their purest state—anger, joy, sadness, fear, excitement. We don't create stories around them or add meaning to them; we simply feel.

We have all seen children laugh, get sad, and get angry without inhibition. We've heard babies cry when they need something or coo while someone is holding them. Within a few months of age, children feel and express a range of emotions, from anger when their bottle is pulled away to sadness, fear, and rejection when their parent isn't present, and happiness when the parent returns.

How our parents respond or react to our emotions sets the template for how we "do" emotions for the rest of our lives. If you are an adult who does not feel your emotions fully, you were not born this way. You were taught and learned not to feel. If you were shamed for your emotions, had parents who tried to "fix" your emotions, or had parents who did not express their own emotions in healthy ways, this becomes your road map for your emotional experience as an adult. Recall Sara's story from the introduction. She often felt numb and discovered that she had learned to suppress her emotions in childhood because her mother would erupt in anger any time Sara cried. If this is something you're experiencing, you have to learn how to unlock, stop numbing, and get curious about your emotions to allow them to flow again. We'll dedicate more time to this in chapter 6, "I Feel My Emotions."

EXERCISE

1. What were you taught about emotions in your home growing up? Was it safe to cry, to be angry, to be sad?

2. Were you supported while having emotions? Was anyone there with you while you experienced emotions?

3. What do you do with your emotions today? Are you connected with and aware of them? Do you allow yourself to feel and process emotions, or do you instead want to numb them?

4. How do you see your childhood experiences of emotions show up in your life today?

5. As an adult, do you share your emotions with anyone else in a healthy way?

2. Needs

All humans have emotional needs; this is normal and healthy. Needs are not the same things as wants. We may want a car or a home or ice cream, but what we need is someone to tell us that we are lovable. Or we may need to feel safe or to know that we matter. True emotional needs might sound like:

- "I need a hug."
- "I need you to sit with me while I cry."
- "I need to hear that you love me, and that I am okay."
- "I need you to hold me, because I hurt myself and need consoling."
- "I need to feel safe."

Healthy adults are in touch with their needs and know how to ask others to meet their needs or how to meet them themselves.

Parents who are not in tune with their children's needs, or who are unable to meet their needs, or worse yet, who shame their children for having needs, teach their children to be "needless." These children often turn into adults who discount or disconnect from what they need.

Being in touch with our needs is something so many of us have to work on. When I ask my clients to name their emotional needs, I more often than not get a blank stare and a response like "I don't know what I need." Does this sound familiar to you?

A client of mine, Carly, was often angry with her partner,

Terry, because Terry never told her how he felt. She would tell him that she loved him, and he would just smile and say thank you. She would give him the silent treatment for a few days, and then she would say she was fine and try to let it go, until the same thing would happen a month later.

"This sounds draining," I said.

Carly said, "No kidding it's draining! If he would just tell me how he felt, it wouldn't have to be this way!"

I responded, "The draining part is not about him; it's how you give him the silent treatment! Putting up a wall of energy and blocking another human for hours and days is exhausting! What do you really need from him?"

"I need to hear that he cares for me and is in this for the long haul."

"Have you asked him directly about that?"

Carly said, "Yes! I asked him to express himself."

"That statement is way too general. This needs to be a direct conversation with him where you ask specifically for what you need. It would be something like this: 'Terry, I love you and can imagine a future with you. I need to know how you feel about us and our future together. Can you please share that with me?'"

Carly said, "Dang, Michelle, that *is* direct."

I replied, "Yep, but this is how healthy adults communicate and get their needs met. They ask for what they need directly."

She left and came back the following week with a huge smile on her face. "I asked for what I needed! And Terry said he loved me and wanted to have a future with me and planned to propose in the next year! We didn't have to fight about it, and I feel so much better in our relationship now that my emotional needs are being met."

By getting in touch with her true needs—the needs that come from the Child Chair—Carly was able to stop the cycle of conflict with Terry and get everything she needed in her relationship.

Our needs can feel out of reach or foreign to us. Maybe we feel guilty or wrong for even having them! Ask yourself: What do you need? Is there a need not being met in your life right now?

EXERCISE

1. How often did you express your needs growing up and have someone tend to them?

2. How in touch with your needs are you now, as an adult?

3. How often do you reach out to others for help?

4. Do you feel that having needs is a sign of weakness?

5. Do you feel guilty or wrong for having needs?

3. Vulnerability

Have you ever seen a child throw a temper tantrum in a store or restaurant? They are screaming at the top of their lungs, causing a scene, and they couldn't care less how others perceive them. You can't get more vulnerable than that. How the parent responds in these situations is important to the child's development. If the child is shamed, spanked, or yelled at repeatedly, they may shut down their vulnerability.

I remember when my kids threw tantrums in public, and as a parent, it was embarrassing! We want to do whatever it takes to calm them down. But rather than shutting them down by shaming them for something they developmentally cannot yet control, it's much healthier to respond to the child's vulnerability by asking what they need and teaching them to use their words to express this (with healthy consequences if they don't). This teaches a child it's okay to be vulnerable, and that there are appropriate times, places, and methods for expressing vulnerability. Growing up, how did your parents respond to expressions of emotions in general as well as your sadness, fears, and emotions like grief? Were you made fun of or told to shut up? Did you feel comfortable crying in front of your parents? Did your siblings bully you when you cried and call you a "crybaby"?

When a child reaches for a parent to console them when they are hurt, it is another form of vulnerability. They have a need and want to have the need met. Some parents respond with shame or saying they are too busy for us, which teaches us to turn off our vulnerability and not trust that people can be there for us. To reach for another and be met with love and kindness helps us to keep our vulnerability alive. Being vulnerable can feel scary—it's opening up to someone else, and their response is out of our control—but when we do and our needs are met, it's an opportunity for connection and growth.

In order to learn healthy vulnerability, we must have an environment of safety growing up. In the beginning of the chapter, I introduced Mary Ann. As she sat in the Child Chair and unpacked how unstable her home life had felt growing up, I gently pointed out that her current anxiety and feelings of fear were coming from this road map that was formed in early childhood, from her parents fighting and her mother threatening to leave, which sent shock waves of fear through her nervous system. Her vulnerability was met with shame and suppression, and this response eventually led her to stop expressing her emotions altogether, resulting in a constant state of anxiety and fear.

In the months to come, after we worked together to update her road map and I provided tools to help her to stay present, relax, and rework her nervous system, Mary Ann was able to live a much calmer and much less anxious life.

EXERCISE

1. How does the word "vulnerable" make you feel? Do you think it's weak to be vulnerable?

2. How willing are you to express your heart, your feelings, and your needs to others? Does it feel safe to do this?

3. How was vulnerability demonstrated or modeled in your growing-up years? Were your family members vulnerable with one another? Was it made fun of or was it a normal way of life within your family?

4. What happened when you were growing up when you shared your emotions or needs? Did you get yelled at, made fun of, or embraced? Was it safe to share with others?

5. What do you do when someone is vulnerable with you, when they share their emotions, tears, or even joy? Does it feel uncomfortable and you want it to stop, or do you connect with their vulnerability?

4. Intimacy

Children naturally long for connection and intimacy with those around them, especially their caregivers. Think about the earlier example of a child who has gotten hurt. What do they want? The closeness and comfort of a parent (maybe a hug or some snuggles) and to know someone is there for them.

When their parent brings them into their arms and lets the child know that it's going to be okay, the child experiences vulnerability (reaching for parent) and intimacy (the hug and consolation from parent). Both needs are met, and the child feels comfortable with them both. In addition to this, the child experiences healthy secure attachment (I can reach for you and you are there for me) as well as trust (I can trust that you are available and willing to console me).

Unfortunately, many parents are not fully present or

struggle with intimacy themselves. When their child comes to them needing a hug or soothing words, they may become rigid (stiff and uncomfortable) and push the child away or try to "fix" it without being fully present. The child then learns that intimacy is unsafe and unneeded, and that vulnerability is not okay, unsafe, or bad. They may even experience shame and shut down intimacy and vulnerability altogether.

EXERCISE

1. Think about your current life. How do you feel about vulnerability and intimacy?

2. Now think back to your childhood. Did you receive physical intimacy from your family members, like hugs or kisses? A pat on the back or a hand on your knee or shoulder if you were upset or needed consoling? Healthy physical touch is intimate. What was this like for you while growing up?

3. When you reached out for a hug or consolation, how did your parents respond?

4. As an adult, do you reach out to others when you need consolation? Does healthy physical touch feel comfortable to you? Does it feel safe and natural?

5. What types of intimacy from your parents did you witness while growing up? Did your parents show affection for each other?

5. Passion

Have you ever seen a child want to play with something over and over again? They may sit for hours and play with Legos or dolls or want to dance all day or do gymnastics. At the age of three, my nephew would hit golf balls in the backyard for hours at a time. He loved to golf and still does at age twenty-one. This is called passion, and we first experience it from the ages of zero to six.

I have had countless clients say that they struggle with passion. Some lack passion in their relationships, in their career, or even in life. When I hear this, I immediately know that feeling numb to these things indicates a "lost child" who needs to be connected with. With help to connect with their inner child, they begin to get glimpses and clues about their passions.

EXERCISE

1. What did you love when you were young? What were your interests? What did you love to play and do?

2. Did your parents support your passions, or did they want you to do or be passionate about something else?

3. Are you living a life with passion now? How so? What things excite you that you are not doing?

4. What needs to change for you to begin to live a life ever more connected to your passions? Are you willing to take the steps necessary to live with more passion in your life?

5. Close your eyes and take a deep breath. Imagine a younger you sitting next to you—the younger you who felt as though they had the world in front of them and they could do anything. Ask that part of you what they would like to do for fun. Dialogue with that part of you and gain clarity on how they feel about your current life and some things that they would like to do that you are not currently doing. Our inner children hold so much information about our passions, and having a conversation with them about it can open up a whole new future!

6. Creativity, Play, and Fun

For the first six years, children live in a world of creative exploration and imagination.

Learning to crawl and walk helps them to explore and engage in fun. Running through mud puddles, finger painting, building with blocks, playing sports, and going to the playground with friends are all forms of healthy creativity, play, and fun.

When a child is allowed the space to be a child, these qualities quite naturally develop, and the child begins to learn what they like and don't like and how to create fun through play and creativity. Unfortunately, many issues can arise that inhibit, block, or suppress the child's natural tendency to want to explore, play, and have fun, which we will discuss later in this chapter.

When we connect with the energy of our inner child, we

will find that other qualities of the Child Chair begin to manifest within our life. For example, when you begin to have more fun and play in your life, you may find that you become more curious about your emotions and needs. When you get curious about your emotions and begin to explore them, feel them, and process them, you may find yourself feeling more vulnerable and sharing with others.

There is an energy to each chair, and the energy of the Child Chair contains all of the qualities mentioned above: emotions, needs, vulnerability, intimacy, passion, and creativity and fun. By activating one quality of the chair, you can open up the energy for other qualities to activate as well, even if you are not "practicing" them. I saw this firsthand with my client Shannon.

When Shannon first arrived, she was friendly and polite but guarded. She sat on my couch and asked for help with finding her passion and purpose in life. "I have a great job that pays well, but life just feels boring," she said. She also shared that she wanted a relationship but was having a hard time finding someone.

I started by taking her through a short, guided session of breathwork and relaxation. I then invited her to drop her attention and awareness "below her chin" into her body and to think about her current job. "How does thinking about your job make you feel emotionally and physically?" I asked.

She sat for a moment then reported that her body felt tight and heavy. I asked if she could get curious and check in on whether she was feeling any emotions as well. She opened her eyes, looked at me, and said, "Sad." She looked a bit shocked. "Also, afraid. Wow, I did not anticipate those emotions. I didn't know I was sad and afraid; I thought I felt numb."

I explained that our true emotions are underneath what we "think" in the mind. When we get access to our true emotions in the body and from the Child Chair, magic happens, and change can occur.

"This will be your homework assignment," I continued. "Practice exactly what we just did here today for at least two minutes a day, and more if you'd like. This practice will connect you more deeply with your inner child. The clearer the connection you have with her, the clearer your life path will become. You will begin to have a deeper understanding of your next steps and so much more."

I worked with Shannon for two months, and she diligently practiced her homework. At the end of two months, she came in a different person. She was far less guarded and more open. She smiled more and even laughed; she had come so far from her first session.

"Something is happening, Michelle." She took a breath. "I am having these recurring thoughts and visions about something that I used to do as a kid. I had forgotten these memories, but they keep coming back to me. I used to bake with my mom when I was growing up. I had an Easy-Bake Oven, and I loved to bake with that and also with my mom and my grandmother. So, I have started to bake and experiment with baking, and I love it. In fact, it's all I think about. What is happening to me? Why these memories?"

"When we reconnect with our inner child, we are 'activating' the energy of the child," I shared. "All kinds of ideas, inspirations, and thoughts will begin to emerge."

"I have also been reaching out to some friends that I had lost touch with and grabbing dinner and coffee," Shannon said. "All that I am doing is checking in daily with my emotions, and all of these other things are happening in my life. My life is completely changing! It's wild."

"This is the power of the connection with our inner child," I told her. "All aspects of the child begin to emerge in our lives. You are practicing one aspect of the child—your emotions—but you are experiencing passion, creativity, and fun, the desire to connect and have fun with friends, and you are honoring your need for connection, which is another inner child quality. All aspects of the inner child are coming through you now, and you have only just begun!"

EXERCISE

1. What did you like to do when you were a kid?

2. As an adult, what do you do for fun? Do you play?

3. These days, where do you experience your creativity flowing through you? Maybe it's playing a sport, attending a dance class, gardening, cooking, practicing yoga, or enjoying another creative pastime. How much time do you make for these activities in your life now?

4. Can you create more time in your day or week for creativity, play, and fun?

Wounding That Occurs in the Child Chair

Earlier in the chapter, we discussed the way that children absorb everything but do not yet have the skills to discern if something is right or wrong based solely on what they've observed. Because we are so vulnerable in this stage of development, and because we form most of our life's road map here, wounding can occur easily and it will impact how we live the rest of our lives, until we decide to take a closer look and heal it.

There are many ways that wounding occurs in childhood and goes on to impact our lives. Let's look at a few of the most common ways below.

Projection Versus Reflection

It's easy for parents to fall into projecting their wants and desires onto their child instead of listening, watching, and understanding who their child is and then reflecting the child's own passions back to them. Maybe you can remember your parents projecting some of their hopes and dreams onto you, and you always felt as if you were falling short. Maybe they pushed you toward a field of study or a career that was important to them but didn't align with your passion.

If you are a parent, this is a good moment to pause and think about how you might be projecting onto your kids. Many years ago, my neighbor Marie's daughter, Gigi, was getting ready to start kindergarten. She was going to take the bus to school and was thrilled about it. Marie, however, was terrified for her to take the bus. She was worried that Gigi would get bullied and that she wouldn't be able to find her way to the kindergarten classroom.

Every time I saw Marie, she would say how nervous she was for Gigi's first day. One day, I finally asked if she had been afraid to take the bus when she was a child. She said, "Yes, I was terrified! I got picked on by my older brother's friends and couldn't find my way to my classroom and got lost. I was so shy then, and I didn't know how to ask anyone for help. I wound up crying and sitting in the hallway until the principal found me and helped me to class. It was awful!"

I told her it was understandable she would be nervous that Gigi might have the same negative experience, then asked her if Gigi seemed afraid at all. She said, "No, she is excited to take the bus and go to school. She is so much more independent and fearless than I ever was!"

Based on what she shared with me, it sounded like she was projecting her fears from her own experience onto Gigi. I let her know that my experience of Gigi was that she was thrilled to go and ride the bus. Marie said, "Michelle, you are so right! I am definitely projecting on her! Any advice?"

"Instead of putting your fear on her, get excited with her and reflect her courage, enthusiasm, and eagerness to go to school!"

Marie did that, and Gigi had a great first day and loved riding the bus. When Gigi got home from her first day, Marie told Gigi how brave she was and how much she admired her confidence—beautiful qualities to reflect back to Gigi as she was in the developmental stage of building her self-image.

When using reflection with children, focus on reflecting *who the child is* rather than what they did, what they look like, how well they performed, or who you want them to become. It's important to validate internal qualities, not just external ones.

For example, even though we want to praise a child when they accomplish something like getting good grades or winning a game, if all the praise is tied to these external accomplishments, it can be easy for a child to only hear that they are smarter than everyone else in their class or the best at a sport. Then, when they leave school or stop playing the sport, they may not know who they are outside of these things that once brought them validation.

Instead, praising the actions that show their internal qualities, like "I love that you helped your brother pick up his toys without me asking; you are thoughtful," or "I love how you hugged your sister when she was crying; you are very caring," can give better reflections of a child's inner character than simply praising how they perform or what they accomplish (though these things are worth celebrating too!).

EXERCISE

1. Do you feel that your parents supported you and your choices growing up, or did they steer you in a way that was pleasing to them?

2. How much input or "guidance" did your parents share with you while growing up?

3. As you look back now, did your parents reflect well who you were?

Fear and Worry

Wounding can also come when we experience fear and worry from our parents. Some parents fear their child will get hurt or sick, causing them to become overprotective. These kids might miss out on experiences that might be uncomfortable at first but that ultimately would expose the child to new things and help build resilience.

Some parents might limit who their kids can play with out of worry for a kid's safety or what they might be exposed to. This may impede the child from developing necessary social skills for later in life, or the child may interpret that play is not okay or that other kids, people, or even the world are unsafe. These limiting beliefs suppress the child's natural desire to play, connect, and have fun.

EXERCISE

1. Did you experience the emotions of fear and worry from your parents as you grew up?

2. If you did, how does this show up in your current life?

3. If you have chronic worry and fear now, what can you do to incorporate more trust? Do you need to ask for what you need? Set clearer boundaries with someone?

Chaos and Drama

Some children live in households that are filled with drama and chaos. Children who grow up like this will find that their nervous system will program itself to run "hot," or fast. If people in your home were unreliable or unpredictable and you had to live on high alert, this becomes your norm.

When you leave your childhood home, your nervous system will still run hot. Being calm feels unnatural to you. You will unconsciously create drama or chaos in your life or in your relationships to feel normal, even if "normal" is hurting you and those around you. You can't help it; your road map that you created early on is telling you this is the right way to act.

If you have chronic anxiety, consider looking into nervous system regulation techniques in order to bring yourself back to balance. Practicing slow, deep breathing is a great place to start, as well as meditation, yoga, and being around others who have a calm, balanced nervous system.

EXERCISE

1. What was life like in your household while growing up? Did you feel that life was relatively peaceful and calm, or was there a lot of drama or chaos?

2. How did this affect you while growing up? How did you compensate for it?

3. Where do you see the effects of chaos and drama in your current life? How does your nervous system function now compared to in your childhood?

Parentification of Children

Another way that the natural development and key qualities of being a child are extinguished happens when the child is overburdened with adult responsibilities, like taking care of a sibling or another child, cleaning the house, cooking, or even consoling or caretaking the parent and managing their emotional and physical needs.

This level of responsibility creates confusion, as the child must abandon parts of their developmental phase to act as an adult for their parent. The "parentified child" is caught in a role reversal, where the child becomes the adult or caretaker, and this situation can have lasting effects on the child as they mature into an adult.

Anxiety, depression, codependency, relationship issues, fatigue, and issues with unexplained exhaustion are all common problems that can result from taking on the role of caretaking or parenting your parent at too young of an age. You might also face issues around identity and knowing who you are.

When our focus is on the needs of others in our earlier years, speaking up for our own needs, sharing what we want (and don't want), and setting healthy boundaries as adults can feel awkward and even make us feel guilty for speaking up for ourselves. Instead, we stay quiet and try to remain needless and wantless. All of this, of course, sets the groundwork for unhealthy relationships of all kinds.

Doing work around building an identity and reconnecting with the true self is a wonderful place to start. We begin to do this by simply turning inward and getting to know what we like and don't like. Journaling about it. Spending time with a safe person, and sharing our likes and dislikes with them.

Inner child work is an excellent process to embark on as it promotes healing for the overburdened child self that missed out on their childhood and helps with building a new identity. You can access a free resource to get you started on my website: theadultchair.com/innerchild.

The bottom line is this: With the right help and tools, you can change, heal, and transform. You just need the desire to do so.

EXERCISE

1. Were you given adult responsibilities as a child? If yes, how so?

2. Did either of your parents lean on you emotionally or physically (for instance, asking you to cook or clean the house or do other "adult tasks")?

3. In what ways did you have to act like an adult while you were growing up? Did one of your parents need you in

ways that they should have leaned on another adult for? Did you have to make adult decisions in any way as a child?

Neglect and Abandonment

Children who have been neglected or abandoned feel the effects across many areas of their lives. Depending on the severity, this can be very traumatizing for a child. They may lose connection with their desire to be creative or play. They may feel lost or alone and try hard to become someone they think their parents want them to be, losing their true selves in the process. They might act out, hoping their parents will "see" or acknowledge it, in order to get love, attention, and connection from their parents.

Neglect isn't always intentional. Overwhelmed parents may not have the bandwidth or patience to manage a baby or a child. They may neglect their children out of pure exhaustion or because they don't have the coping skills for a crying baby or screaming toddler.

Overwhelmed and emotionally dysregulated parents may also get triggered into anger or rage at their children. This could cause the child to disconnect from their emotions and needs and numb out, so they don't feel the fear and pain from their parents.

If you grew up experiencing any form of abandonment or neglect, you may experience a heightened nervous system that feels on high alert. You may have issues with emotional regulation, anger, and rage, or feel disconnected from your emotions. ADHD, impulse control, hyperactivity, and even memory impairment or learning difficulties can be the result of neglect and abandonment.

Many people who grow up feeling low self-worth often fear others will abandon them, which causes attachment wounding and leads to relationship issues later in life. They may find that either they don't want people to get too close and so keep others at a "safe" distance, or they feel anxious when alone and want others (or their partner) to be close all the time and feel anxious when they are away from them. Yet others may feel a mix of both anxiety when their partner is away and a sense of overwhelm when they return, flooded with tension when their partner is close again, and wanting to create distance.

Practicing each of the five pillars (in part 2 of this book) can be extremely helpful in healing from neglect and abandonment. Learning to feel your emotions, practicing self-compassion, building self-worth, doing trigger work, and setting boundaries are exactly the foundational tools necessary to rebuild the self.

Inner child work is also an incredible tool to incorporate for those who have experienced childhood abandonment or neglect. See page 244 for the link to that resource.

EXERCISE

1. Was neglect or abandonment part of your growing-up years? If yes, how so?

2. How do you feel that this experience is still playing out in your adult life?

    a. As you read through the consequences of neglect and abuse above, do you feel that you exhibit any of those in your life now?

    b. If so, write about them. We must own our reality in order to become free to shift and transform. It's the first step (and the first pillar) on your healing journey. Be honest here. No judgment, just the facts.

3. Close your eyes and imagine the younger you that felt neglected or abandoned, even if in a small way. Turn toward that younger you and let them know that you will never leave or abandon them. Let them know that you are here with them, and you want to get to know them better. Commit to spending time with this part of yourself at least once a week in a visualization session. Even for just a few minutes, once a week, this can be a powerful healing for abandonment wounding.

Childhood wounding is traumatic. Trauma is defined as any distressing event that causes long-lasting effects. Many of us have, unfortunately, experienced very deep trauma, but I can't think of anyone, not even a child, who has not experienced trauma on some level. A goldfish dying could be a distressing event to a child. When my son left his favorite blanket at a hotel when we were on vacation—the blanket that he carried with him all day and slept with—it was traumatic for him.

The good news is that with the tools and processes within this model, even much deeper trauma that occurred while growing up can be not only corrected but healed. In the next section, we will go over exactly how to do that using the inner child.

How to Re-parent and Heal Your Inner Child

In this chapter, we've used the Child Chair to explore which of the key qualities of development you might feel you're lacking, and we've looked at childhood wounds that might have caused that lack.

If you are reading this and realize that you feel disconnected from various qualities of the Child Chair, perhaps from your passion, or from feeling your emotions, or from feeling connected to your needs, please don't feel discouraged. Throughout the rest of the book, I will teach you what you need to do in order to "re-parent" yourself and reclaim the lost or underdeveloped parts from this phase.

This is what is so beautiful: With the correct processes, you are able to correct, reprogram, and heal the younger parts of you with this model. Regardless of what happened in your past, inner child work is a way to "update" the outdated or dysfunctional programming that you inherited or learned mistakenly from your parents.

Let me share an example of what this looked like for me. One Saturday afternoon, I was running around doing errands. I had to return a bunch of items, and I felt this dragging resistance inside of me, a sort of heaviness. I decided to check in with my inner child to see how she was doing.

I pulled into a parking space at Target, turned toward the passenger seat, and imagined the younger version of myself sitting there. I closed my eyes and asked little Michelle how she was doing.

She crossed her arms and looked out the passenger window. She wouldn't look at me. I asked her what was wrong. She peered over her shoulder at me and with a sneer said, "I'm bored. I hate errands."

I laughed to myself and asked little Michelle, "What would you like to do instead?"

She said, "I want ice cream!"

Here is the crazy thing: I, adult Michelle, do not like ice cream!

In that moment, I realized the magic of doing this work and how these inner, younger versions of us are alive and have preferences and emotions. It also validated the importance of connecting with them.

"Ice cream, huh? Well, what if we finish errands and then we go to Jeni's Ice Cream?"

In my mind, she spun her head around to me. "Really?"

I smiled. "Yep."

She smiled back. "Okay, let's go to Target!"

I checked in with myself and noticed I felt a new lightness, and the heaviness was gone. A smile came over my face, and the next hour of errands was somehow fun!

An hour later, as promised, "we" went to Jeni's Ice Cream and got the salted peanut butter with chocolate. And, I must admit, it was delicious!

As I saw that day in the Target parking lot, there is huge power in connecting with your inner child. When you start to feel disconnected from yourself, bring your attention into your body and tune in to the voice of your inner child. Inner child work is a game changer for activating your emotions, needs, intimacy, vulnerability, and so much more. It is also a great way to identify and work through triggers, which we will cover in chapter 7.

EXERCISE

Let's walk through an exercise together with five ways to help you reconnect with your inner child.

1. **Connect to your younger self through your emotions.**

   Throughout the day, turn your attention toward yourself and, with curiosity, ask yourself, "How do I feel?" Then wait for the answer to come. You may hear an emotion word like "lonely" or "happy," or you may hear nothing. If you don't hear anything, that's okay! You must be patient with yourself and give this time. Once you learn how to make contact with yourself, this will become easier.

Sometimes, you may simply feel a sensation in your body, such as a knot or flutter or openness. This is also a perfectly fine way to feel your emotions.

This process helps to activate the energy (or energize) the child within you. The more energy within the child, the easier this process becomes and the more bonded you become with this part of you.

2. **Ask, "What do I need?"**
Close your eyes and ask yourself this question: "What do I need?" Some of us (especially us codependents and people pleasers) grow up taking care of others, and focusing on ourselves and our needs feels awkward or even selfish. But remember, a need is different from a want. Think of emotional needs, such as "I need a hug," or "I need someone to listen to me vent," or "I need to feel like I matter." By asking yourself this question, you will be activating the energy of the inner child.

3. **Act like a child!**
Ask yourself, "What would be fun?" And do it! Finger paint, draw, jump in a mud puddle, whatever sounds like pure fun to you!

4. **Write to your inner child.**
If you could go back in time as the adult you are today and speak to the younger you, what would you say? Would you let them know the truth about your parents or siblings? Maybe you could tell them you made it and you grew up into an adult? How about telling them how much you love

them and you know how hard it was at times? As if they are a pen pal, write to them and tell them anything on your heart. Tell them how amazing they are, that you have missed them, that you look forward to getting to know them, or anything at all.

You can also ask them a question by writing it with your dominant hand, then answering with your nondominant hand. This is a wonderful way to get the energy flowing and connected from your Adult to your inner child.

5. **Sit with your Child and check in.**

When you feel "off," anxious, sad, or any other strong emotion, check in with your inner child. I also love to do this when I am not emotional. My story in the previous section about getting ice cream is a good example of how casual this can look.

Close your eyes and take a few long, deep, slow breaths. When you are ready, imagine your younger self, your child self, next to you or in front of you. You may see, hear, feel, or sense your inner child. Always go with the first thing that comes to your mind. All are perfect.

When you feel, see, or sense your Child, ask them how they are doing. Let them know you are here with them and are happy to see them. Introduce yourself, letting them know that you are the grown-up version of them and telling them how many years old you are now.

Let them know that you'd like to get to know them better. Ask them anything you wish, and wait for a response. You will get one. Go with the first thought that you have. Don't second-guess this; go with the voice that comes to you.

Spend time talking with them and getting to know them. What would you say to an actual little kid if they were sitting in front of you? Try questions like:

- How do you feel?
- Is there anything you need?
- Would you like to play?

Then imagine coloring or playing with dolls or action figures. You can imagine going to the park or the beach or playing in the snow. Make up whatever feels fun! Ask your Child what they want to do—you will more than likely be surprised.

If your Child is not interested in connecting with you, or even if they're angry with you, it's okay. Maybe they feel abandoned or sad or mad because you have never connected with them before. It's fine! Let them know that you'll be back the next day and check in again.

They may play hard to get in the beginning to see if you are really going to show up for them. Continue to check in until they connect with you. In my twenty-five years of helping people with inner child work, I have never had the experience of an inner child not eventually wanting to connect.

This process activates the connection between your adult self and your child self. You may connect with various ages of your Child. One day, it may be your two-year-old who shows up, and one day it may be your six-year-old. Go with whoever shows up for you and know it's perfect.

This process may take a few minutes or longer. Go with what feels right for you. This is a wonderful daily practice to do day or night.

Inner child work creates a new feeling of aliveness within. You will find that you are more connected with your emotions, needs, and all of the qualities of the Child Chair.

You will also feel a deeper connection with "self." Self-compassion becomes easier and a more natural way of being. You'll experience a new relationship with yourself, a deeper connection to you! This connection will cultivate deeper self-respect and love.

Enjoy cultivating a new relationship with this precious part of you, and you'll find yourself growing a new inner connection that you didn't feel was possible before.

∽

Children are born with unlimited potential. Even if you didn't get everything you needed as a child, it's not too late to become everything you were meant to be. As the healthy adult you are becoming today, you can re-parent your inner child and let them bloom into whoever they are here to be! We can get back to that childlike passion and experience play, delight, vulnerability, and intimacy, and when we do it from the perspective of our Adult Chair, it's a beautiful thing!

But before we can become healthy adults, we also have to go through the adolescent stage of development.

Around age seven, we journey into our next phase, the Adolescent Chair. This essential time of our development can be challenging, as our ego is in full swing, and our sense of self is continuing to form. The road map that was created from all of our lessons in the Child Chair is now in place, and our ego uses this to navigate our path forward, not only through adolescence but through the rest of our lives!

In the next chapter, let's slide over into the Adolescent Chair.

CHAPTER TWO

The Adolescent Chair

————————— ⌒ —————————

Marin came in for a session and wanted help with being too "easygoing." She shared that her boyfriend, Theo, was annoyed that she never had any opinions on where they went out to eat, what movies to see, weekend plans, or even travel.

Marin said that she really didn't care what they did, and that she loved Theo's ideas. She considered herself easygoing, fun, and free. After further probing, she shared that her older sister had been really difficult for her parents. She was four years older than Marin and gave her parents "a hell of a time" in high school—sneaking out, doing drugs, everything her parents asked her not to do. She caused a lot of chaos and drama in the house.

Her parents praised Marin for how "easy" she was and thanked her all the time for listening so well and not rocking the boat in the family. Because of this, she took on the mask of the "good girl" and people pleaser. She went with the flow, did what she was told, and did not rock the boat. She hardly asked for anything from middle school until she left home.

I helped Marin to understand that this was a strategy that her ego developed to help her fit into her family, and that it was unhelpful and unnecessary now as a thirty-year-old woman.

I started asking Marin questions about her favorite foods, movies, and everyday things in life. It was uncomfortable at first, and her ego was pushing hard against this idea. I reassured her that it was okay to speak up for what she liked and what felt good to her.

Slowly but surely, she began to get in touch with what was important for and to her *and* to speak up about it.

With time, she found that it got easier, and it actually felt good to get what she wanted, go to the restaurant that she wanted, and vacation where she wanted. Marin realized that it was safe to speak up and share her opinions, *and* it was also nice to be easygoing at times. She discovered that she could be both—an easygoing woman with opinions. It also helped improve her relationships, not only with Theo, but also with her family, friends, and work colleagues, as she showed up more fully and authentically.

Like Marin, we all have an ego that tries to keep us safe and that adopts strategies (however unproductive they might be) to protect us. This is a hallmark of the adolescent stage of development and the source of so many of the common issues people face.

In the last chapter, we covered how our earliest years, our Child Chair, created a road map that we follow for the rest of our lives. In this chapter, we will go over what happens during the Adolescent Chair developmental phase of our lives and how it affects us now as adults.

We'll explore the ego, false self, and masks that we wear to stay connected, safe, and alive, as well as common indicators that you might still be living in your Adolescent Chair. To make it easier to identify, the end of the chapter offers a reflection exercise to help you discover your hidden Adolescent running the show behind the scenes.

By the time you get to the end of this chapter, you will have a much greater understanding of why you do what you do and how to get unstuck so you can start living as your healthiest adult self . . . the you that you truly are today!

What Is the Adolescent Chair?

Around age six or seven until around age twenty-five, we move into the Adolescent Chair. This phase includes preadolescence, adolescence, and postadolescence. This is when so much of our self-image, self-esteem, and self-concept are formed. It's also, importantly, when our ego drives us to make decisions and act from fear-based strategies in order to survive.

As we make the transition from Child Chair to Adolescent Chair, you might be wondering, how do we go from pure emotions and pure needs as a child to living with masks and personas as an adolescent?

As we learned in the previous chapter, as children, we are constantly taking in information, learning about the world, and forming beliefs and a road map for life. Then, when ego comes online, it uses this information to develop survival strategies to help it navigate through this road map. Can you imagine attempting to travel from where you live now to a destination with only a paper map that was created when you were six years old? This is how we live in our Adolescent Chair!

When we enter into this phase at age six, we are still young and 100 percent reliant on our parents for food, shelter, rides to and from places, protection from others, and direction on how to live—not to mention love, consolation, emotional support, and guidance on how to navigate our emotions and live a successful, healthy, peaceful life.

Our understanding of the world is still developing and immature, but with the ego now online and taking over our decisions, we use our road map to develop fear-based strategies to help us stay connected and safe in our families—and as we get older, in our social groups. These strategies become our way of life, our new beliefs about how to exist in the world. These beliefs get programmed into us as if we were computers, and we live by them without realizing they are limiting beliefs and programs that cover up our true selves.

I once had three unrelated male clients who were all raised by very similar abusive, alcoholic fathers. They were all burned with their fathers' cigarettes, called losers, and told that they were not wanted.

Each one became unbelievably successful, drove big cars, and made boatloads of money. They were all built like body-builders as well.

While I worked with all three of them, it was fascinating to see how their egos had driven them to build up a "strong" false self as a way to survive their fathers' abuse and their childhoods. Their strategy was to rely on no one, protect themselves, and defend themselves. The problem is the strategies that worked when they were kids to gain approval, affection, love, and safety often didn't work anymore as adults.

Maybe you've seen this in your own life. Ever catch yourself getting into dysfunctional relationship after dysfunctional relationship and can't figure out why?

Ever wonder why you married someone just like your mother, even when you swore you wouldn't?

Ever feel emotionally exhausted from caretaking everyone around you, or feel anxious from perfectionism, or wonder why you can't move forward in life?

Chances are these are outdated strategies that your ego developed from your outdated childhood road map. The good news is that it can be updated!

Before we get to how to do that, we need to understand what the ego is and how it often takes over in our decision-making process, even when it's working from outdated programming.

The Development of the Ego

The adolescent phase is marked by the development of the ego. The ego is our earthly mind that lacks a higher perspective. It is rooted in fear, and its job is to keep us safe and alive. This is a good and noble goal, and it does everything it can to keep us connected, accepted, and loved, but sometimes that comes at the expense of who we truly are. We become whoever we need to be in order to fit in, instead of being our authentic selves.

When we are born, we are the most authentic version of ourselves, because we understand where we have come from: Source / God / divine light (choose the term or belief that most resonates with you). We feel connected to and part of this magnificent energy.

Then, we arrive here, and our spiritual self, our soul, takes on a "human suit" in order to experience life. We also attempt to deeply connect and attach with our family.

As we grow up and the ego comes online, we begin to feel further away from this "oneness" and instead feel more and more separate from that feeling of unconditional love / God / Source. In the adolescent phase of life, we start to individuate and try to figure out who we are apart from our families.

This separate feeling—this feeling that you are an individual and not part of the whole—creates fear . . . fear that you have to protect yourself, fend for yourself, and keep yourself alive.

It sounds extreme, but it can look very subtle. When I was growing up, my family, including my extended family, was made up of very emotional, typical Italians. Quite often our house was loud, people yelling about the Sunday football game, yelling about a client that screwed my father over, or sharing some drama happening with my uncle.

I was feeling a lot on the inside, but I had no one to go to. No one had "emotional training" from their parents, so my parents either tried to fix the situation or told me not to cry and that everything was going to be okay.

My mother was my "best friend" and tried her best, but my emotional needs would often turn into my mom and me blaming someone (usually my uncle) for hurting one of us. Or we would just "move on."

Carbohydrates became my go-to emotional support, specifically pizza, pasta, potatoes, and popcorn. I remember at a very young age using those foods to help me feel better. It was like injecting morphine into my system when I ate them. They served as a fantastic emotional support for me, but my craving for these foods became a problem I would have to work through when I started trying to live more out of my Adult Chair.

Because the ego is doing what it can to keep us safe and alive, it cannot live in the moment. It is always living in the past and future, creating stories about why this happened or why So-and-So did that to me, while also creating assumptions about what's coming in my future.

Almost all of the time, our stories and assumptions are inaccurate because of the filters that we are seeing our reality through. They are based on our wounding, not on truth. When we are living in stories and assumptions, we are making decisions and judgments while looking through a distorted lens.

Our ego is quick to judge and react to keep us safe. It is the part of us that makes quick, rash decisions and judgments (of self and others) and has flash anger (or rage). It may blame, gossip, or not take responsibility when at fault (the ego doesn't know how to do this).

This phase is also when our codependency, people-pleasing behaviors, and perfectionism are born. We develop these personas believing that they are who we are. The ego doesn't have the awareness that we are doing this; it is reactive and adopts strategies in order to survive that become personas that feel like our identity. We will explore this process further in the next section.

The Development of Masks

The ego pays attention to how others receive us, and it's driven to fit in, belong, and stay part of the tribe. If we are not part of a tribe or a group, we may get kicked out and die, so the ego does everything it can to ensure we are included, even if it means changing who we are at our core. This is how our pure essence that we were born with, our true self, gets covered up with a false self.

I was incredibly shy growing up. I rode the bus to school, and the older (and cooler) kids sat in the back of the bus. I sat in the front with my best friend every day.

One day, I brought my tape recorder on the bus and was playing music. One of the older kids heard the song—the *Batman* theme song—and yelled at me to turn it up. I can still remember that feeling of the older kids paying attention to me. My face flushed, and I was thrilled and nervous at the same time. Then they asked my friend and me to come back and play more music. We sat in the back of the bus with the older and coolest kids from that day forward.

A week later, I was eating a banana on the bus, and my new friends dared me to throw it out the window at the bus next to us so it would land on the windshield and freak out the bus driver. I (that is, my ego) couldn't resist the opportunity to get attention, so I hurled that banana peel out the window, and it landed squarely on the bus driver's windshield. Both buses stopped.

The incident almost resulted in me getting suspended from my little Catholic school . . . *and* the greatest thing happened: I became one of the cool kids. I was now considered a daredevil. I would do things that others wouldn't do and push limits. I gained attention and admiration for these characteristics. "What a victory!" my ego thought.

The mask that was constructed when I was ten years old lived strong and helped me to fit in throughout high school and college. I was the one who would drink more than others, smoke more, and do the things that would get a reaction out of my friends. When I would hear the words "I dare you to . . . ," that same part of me would light up, just like when I was on the bus.

When we become "someone else" in life, this is what we refer to as putting a mask on. We learn at a young age to put masks on to fit in and feel accepted and loved. Our ego builds these identities, or masks, as we go through the adolescent developmental phase.

Our collection of masks makes up our false self.

During the adolescent period, we are learning who we are

and how we fit into our family, our friend group, and the world. We are experiencing acceptance and love from others but also rejection. This feeling of not fitting in or feeling un-loved drives us to change and to become someone who is ac-ceptable and lovable.

This process separates us more and more from who we truly are—our true selves.

As an adult and parent, I saw this development of the mask in my son Graham when he moved to a new school in eighth grade. He loved the school and was thrilled to be mak-ing friends. One day, he invited James over, and asked him if he'd like to play Legos. This was Graham's favorite thing to do; he had been obsessed with building Legos since he could walk.

James looked at him and said, "Legos?" and started laughing. He said, "Dude, Legos are for kids. Do you really play with Legos?"

Graham shifted uncomfortably, then laughed and said, "No, but my little brother does. I hate them. They are for little kids. I used to play when I was young."

That was the day the giant clear bin of Legos was hidden out of sight from any kids coming over. That was the day I saw Graham develop one of his masks and cover up a little bit more of his true self—the part of himself that loved art, Legos, design, and anything creative; his playful, passionate inner child.

We create these masks to fit in and stay connected to oth-ers so we are not ostracized and kicked out of our group. From our ego's perspective, our life depends on it. If we are kicked out of our group, it could result in death, or at least social isolation, so we change who we are.

The Ego, Society, and Expectations

As a twelve-year-old, Graham didn't have an adult perspective yet; he was naturally seated squarely in his Adolescent Chair. He wasn't able to say, "Hey, James, I love Legos, and yes, I'll play as long as I want to." The problem comes when as adults, we let our ego drive decisions from the emotional perspective of an adolescent. In fact, most of us live life based on what society expects us to do instead of living a soul-led life.

Think about how often your decisions are made from fear or from your head instead of your heart.

For example, in the United States (and possibly other countries as well), the "right" way to raise our kids is to get them involved in sports at an early age, get them reading, and push them hard to do more and more—enroll in the honors courses, do travel sports, and take on a thousand other extracurriculars. There is a collective consciousness built around these activities.

It's not only exhausting; it disconnects us from our true self, our soul, and reinforces life in the Adolescent Chair, driven by the ego.

Then we enter into our adult life, get married, have kids, and wake up one day asking ourselves why we are not happy. We did all the "right" things, but we lack joy and can't figure out why.

This is the result of an ego-led life.

What we want to do is to wake up to the fact that we are living this way and make more heart-based choices for ourselves. This is when we move from the head to the heart and begin to live a life aligned with our soul and not the ego mind. This is living out of the Adult Chair. And it's something I saw clearly in my work with my client Cameron.

Cameron came in feeling miserable . . . and guilty for feeling this way. "I have two beautiful children, a husband, and great friends. How can I feel so miserable?"

The more I learned about Cameron, the clearer it was to me why she was miserable. Cameron had four sisters, and they were all very close to their parents. She and her sisters lived within thirty minutes of their parents and spent every Sunday there for dinner.

All of her sisters stayed at home with their children. Cameron's mother had done the same and always told her girls how important it was for a mother to raise her children. She would judge mothers who decided to work and put kids in daycare. She would say, "Daycare is not a place for children. A woman's place is in the home."

Cameron's kids were one and three. She stayed home with them and had a playgroup once a week with their friends. Before she became a mother, she and her two friends had started a successful catering business. She loved to cook and loved owning a business.

When Cameron and her husband decided to have kids, they decided that she would stay home with the kids and step away from the business. Her two friends kept the business going, and it continued to grow and became extremely well known in her town as *the* place to order from. They even opened a storefront.

"How does talking about the business make you feel?" I asked.

She sat for a moment, then said, "I loved everything about that business. It's hard for me to see what my friends have done. I feel a bit jealous and want to be part of it. It was a huge undertaking and risk when we started that business, but right away it grew. I loved everything about it."

"And how do you feel about staying at home with your girls?" I asked.

"I adore my daughters, but I realize that being a stay-at-home mom is a bit boring. I don't feel fulfilled."

I asked if she would want to work with her friends in the business again, and she immediately said, "No way! A woman's place is in the home, and my mother would be furious!"

I reflected to her the enthusiasm in her face and body and how her energy illuminated all around her when she spoke about her business. "This enthusiasm is what happens when you align with your soul, Cameron, and when you are living life on purpose according to your divine plan. When we make decisions from the ego mind, it doesn't feel good. We know we are on the right path by how we feel. Perhaps you are not meant to follow your mom's footsteps, and you are meant to work as well as raise your kids."

She looked perplexed. "How would I ever do that? My mom would disown me."

"Whose life are you living, Cameron?" I asked. "Your life

or your mother's life? Do you really believe that your mom would disown you if you went back to work? Feel into that statement before you answer."

She sat for a moment, then shared, "Well, she would be *very* disappointed and judge me."

"Okay, and what's wrong with that?" I asked. "It will feel uncomfortable, but when you sit in the uncomfortable emotions, they eventually move through you. Then you are left with doing what you want to do. It has nothing to do with not loving your mother; it's simply disagreeing with her opinion and values around how to raise kids. It's okay to do that. The highest and healthiest way to live is with soul alignment and honoring that God/Source connection within. When you make decisions from here, you are honoring yourself, your mother, and your children!"

Over the next two sessions, we learned there was no denying that she was meant to be working with her business. I listened and reflected so she could find her truth and break the ego's idea that she needed to stay at home.

During her third session, she shared that she could not get the business out of her mind. She had shared this with her husband, and even he said he had not seen her more excited about something since having children.

She decided to pitch an idea to her friends that she would work part-time for now, until her kids were in kindergarten, and she would get someone to come to the home to watch them while she worked. This felt reasonable to her, and she was elated.

She was nervous about sharing the news with her mother, so we role-played how it could look, and when she finally told her, she was so clear, enthusiastic, and aligned with her soul that her mother was not nearly as upset as Cameron feared she would be. Cameron had broken free of her ego belief and found her new truth—her higher truth—and she felt complete.

Parts and Personas

During the adolescent phase, we form personas as a strategy to keep us safe, accepted, and alive. With time, these beliefs and programs become part of who we think we are. For Cameron, her attempt to control her mother's anger resulted in her doing what her mother wanted. Cameron didn't know it, but she was unconsciously manipulating a situation to keep everyone calm.

I'm sure you have heard people say, "I am a control freak," or "I know, I know, I'm such a perfectionist." Teenagers easily take on identities like "jock," "nerd," "the smart one," or "the class clown." These are external ways we find to belong in our social groups, and at that age, we build our sense of self around them. Our ego mind does the same thing internally, building an identity around the strategies it's found to keep us safe.

But in life, unlike high school, we don't automatically "graduate" and move on from these identities, or parts, once we reach a certain age. It takes the conscious awareness of our healthy adult self to begin to see these parts for what they are.

Think of your whole self as a puzzle that has hundreds of pieces, which we're calling "parts." When you put the puzzle together, all one hundred plus pieces, it makes up your whole self. Your whole self comprises an inner critic, a judger, a controller, a lover, an inner child, and more. Some of these parts are even centered around beliefs, for example an "I am not worthy" part or an "I am unlovable" part or an "I don't matter" part.

These parts run our lives until we become aware of them. Imagine a little kid driving a school bus with a bunch of kids on it. That's what it's like inside of us! Sometimes our inner critic walks to the front of the bus and takes the wheel, sometimes our victim, sometimes our people pleaser. It's as if all of the parts are at the back of the bus, ready to take their turn at the wheel when needed.

When we develop into a healthy conscious adult and raise our awareness of these parts, our lives begin to change. Waking up to our parts helps us to crack the mask of the false self that we have unconsciously been living with and to rediscover and live from the true self that we were born with.

When we begin the journey of remembering who we are, we take back the reins from the ego, climb back in the driver's seat, regain the balance of both ego mind and heart, and live from a more aware state—and our lives change.

The Adult Chair model teaches you how to hold on to those reins and live from a balanced state, an aware state of mind, and a higher state of consciousness.

Identifying Adolescent Indicators

We cannot change what we do not know. In order to crack the mask of the false self that we unconsciously build and live from, we must raise our awareness of the qualities of the Adolescent Chair. Below is a list of indicators that can tell us when we are living from our unconscious ego mind versus our conscious adult self, or higher mind. See if you recognize your behavior within any of these indicators. The exercise at the end of this chapter is another good way of raising your awareness about how often you might be living out of your Adolescent Chair, rather than your Adult Chair.

When you do find yourself in one of these indicators, do not judge; instead, choose your way out of it. These indicators will help you to notice and become familiar with what it feels like when you are in your Adolescent Chair. Do not beat up on yourself, judge, or blame. Our job right now is to notice and choose a new perspective.

Unconscious: My perspective is limited. I have no awareness or limited awareness of my feelings and thoughts. I think I am my feelings and thoughts. I am reactive because of it. I am not connected to my heart or my body or my higher mind.

Past and future: I am always looking for ways and ideas to keep myself safe. I base this on what I have experienced in the past and project those ideas into the future.

Separate: I am separate from God/Source and alone. I am left here to fend for myself and keep myself safe and alive.

Absolutes or universal quantifiers: I use language like "always," "never," "every time," "everybody," etc. Also known as black-and-white thinking, these words close down my awareness and perspective and limit my options. They also put others on the defensive when used in conversation: "You always treat me like this," or "Everyone knows you are a liar."

"Shoulds": I use the word "should," which is rooted in shame, rather than "could," which comes from my healthy adult self.

Victim mindset: I have a mindset where I see myself as powerless and blame others for my struggles, even when the evidence tells a different story. When I am stuck in this pattern, I might distrust others, avoid owning my part in situations, feel hopeless about my life, and even resent those who seem happy or successful.

Easily triggered: I have a hard time with emotional regulation. I may be quick to anger (or even rage), quick to feel hurt by others, and quick to fall into a victim mindset. I might easily fall into a pattern of feeling sorry for myself and get quiet or broody and stonewall people (give them the silent treatment). I have a hard time letting things go and staying in emotional balance.

Perfectionist: I believe I have to be perfect to be accepted or loved. I can be very hard on myself and beat up on myself.

Gossiper: Gossiping makes me feel better about myself. If I spread "news" about how messed up someone else's life is, my life looks better.

Judger: By judging others, I feel better about myself. Judgment is a way to pump up my own self-image.

Worrier and/or obsessor: I get caught in worry or ruminating thoughts in an attempt to figure out or find reprieve from an internal emotional pain (from the Child Chair).

Avoider: If I pretend something is not happening, it's not real. I distract myself and believe this can prevent me from experiencing emotional pain, embarrassment, or even my own achievements! (The ego likes to keep us in our comfort zone, where it's safe.)

Blocking emotions: I don't know what to do with my emotions. When I experience them in my body, they feel uncomfortable, and I consciously or unconsciously do everything I can to shut them down, block them, or numb them.

How Often Am I Living in My Adolescent Chair?

We all live in our Adolescent Chair sometimes. The goal is to identify the patterns you see yourself falling into often so that you can start to pull yourself into your Adult Chair more easily and more often.

EXERCISE

Below are some typical thoughts and ideas that would come from our Adolescent Chair, or ego. Read each question and answer "true" or "false" to each one. Then tally up the number of times you answered "true," which indicates the amount of time you are spending in your Adolescent Chair.

- I am quick to react.
- I am quick to "fix" problems and issues.
- I feel as if I need to find answers to problems immediately and might obsess until my problems/issues are resolved or taken care of.
- I am not good at being with myself. I find myself keeping busy, being with friends, or distracting myself in some way (TV, phone, social media, etc.) when I am alone and have nothing to do.
- I try to control my environment and other people and like things to be a certain way. Otherwise, I feel unsettled, nervous, or even anxious.
- I use the word "should" a lot.
- I speak with absolutes like "You always do that" or "This happens every time."
- I am not good at seeing my own problems or issues. In fact, I think I am issue-free. I may believe that others have issues, but "I am good."
- I focus a lot on the future or the past. I may have thoughts like "If this would happen, I'd be so much happier" or "If only I had made that decision, I'd be a lot happier now."

- I avoid feeling my emotions. I don't like emotions.
- I avoid confrontation and don't speak up for myself. Boundaries feel foreign to me.
- I tend to blame others for my circumstances. I may blame my parents, siblings, friends, partner, etc. I don't take ownership in my life and believe my issues are due to other people.
- I focus more on the people around me and make sure they are okay before myself. I may feel drained or fatigued.
- I can be defensive and get frustrated or angry quickly. I don't like it when others bring things up to me that I have done wrong. I don't take constructive criticism well.
- I tend to flare up and can get angry quickly. I sometimes may even have rage.
- I gossip or talk about others a little or a lot.
- I am uncomfortable with sharing my vulnerabilities with others.
- I feel as if I can show up like a different person when I am alone compared to when I am with others in my family, among my friends, or at work.
- I have an internal voice(s) that can be very loud or whisper what a loser or bad person I am. This part can be mean and criticize me and make me feel like a fraud.
- I find myself fatigued from feeling as if I have to keep others happy, and others might have joked with me that I am a people pleaser.
- I feel that I am a victim of my circumstances. Others may feel bad for me. Some part of their affirmation feels validat-

ing or even good. I tend to tell others my "story" to gain sympathy from them.

- I am quick to judge myself or others.
- I am not great at waiting and allowing things to unfold. I want answers now.
- I like to move fast and get things done ASAP. I have a lot on my plate, and downtime or relaxation time, when I'm doing nothing, feels lazy to me.
- I may imagine worst-case scenarios. Then I justify my pessimism and say I am a realist and we should be prepared for the worst.

Please do not feel overwhelmed if you are finding yourself mostly in your Adolescent Chair. Instead, celebrate that you can see yourself so well. Once you become aware of your unhealthy beliefs and behaviors, you are well on your way to growing into your healthy adult self. You will find more about how to do this in part 2 of the book, but first, let's examine how a healthy adult develops into living from the Adult Chair.

CHAPTER THREE

The Adult Chair

Gerard came in, sat on my couch, put his head in his hands, and said, "Michelle, I totally messed up, and I am now in the doghouse."

"What happened? Things have been going so well with you and Marcy."

Gerard was a forty-two-year-old divorced father of two. He had been dating Marcy for about four months and was really falling for her.

"Marcy invited me to her friend's birthday party, and I initially said yes, but I had forgotten about the playoff game happening that week. My favorite team made the playoffs, and all my friends were going to the sports bar to watch the game. I didn't want to miss it, but I also didn't know how to tell her because I was afraid she'd be pissed, so the day of her friend's birthday party, I sent her a text a few hours before that I couldn't go and went out with my friends instead. She hasn't talked to me since. That was a week ago, and I really miss her. Can you help me get her back? I really screwed up."

"Gerard, when you think about canceling at the last minute with Marcy, how does it make you feel?"

"Bad. But I honestly felt like I had no options! No matter what I said to her, it wouldn't have been okay."

"Not necessarily, Gerard. You could have had a conversation from your Adult Chair, but instead, you were in your Adolescent Chair." I walked with Gerard step by step through what this looked like, so he could notice it the next time:

1. You waited until the last minute.
2. You texted instead of having a conversation with her.
3. You didn't share the whole story with her. You just said you couldn't go to the party. You are also defending yourself instead of empathizing.
4. You didn't apologize.
5. You didn't compromise with her.

Here is how it could have looked for Gerard from his Adult Chair:

1. The moment you knew that your favorite team was in the playoffs and the game overlapped with her friend's party, you could have had a discussion with her.
2. You would tell her you'd love to watch the game with your friends at your favorite sports bar and apologize for having to cancel.

3. You would ask her if she would be okay with you missing the party and offer to come before or after the game.

4. You could ask how you can make it up to her and let her know that she is important to you.

Gerard acknowledged he could have handled the dilemma better from his Adult Chair and asked what it would look like to repair the relationship from his Adult Chair now. I gave him this list:

1. Drive to Marcy's house and say these things in person. Texting does not work well because we can't feel the tone of the sender.

2. Take responsibility. No excuses or defending. For example, say, "I made a big mistake with how I handled things last week with your friend's birthday party."

3. Apologize and let her know you are very sorry for how you handled things and you will do your best to not let it happen again.

4. Tell her that you would like to repair this and move forward.

5. Ask her what she needs from you in order to move forward.

6. Let her know that you want to do better in the future and ask if she would consider taking you back and coming up with a repair strategy.

Gerard accepted his homework, and after our session, he drove straight to Marcy's house, where she accepted his apology and was pleased that he wanted to find a way to develop healthy, empathetic communication with her.

This chapter is where everything we've learned so far comes together. You will learn more about what the Adult Chair is and how to begin to live in it more often. You will see how it relates to and connects with the other two chairs, and you will gain a clear understanding of when you are in your Adult Chair and when you might have slipped out of it, so that you can find your way back.

We will end with some exercises and daily practices that will help you to grow deeper roots into your Adult Chair so that you stay there on a more regular basis.

What Is the Adult Chair?

At the age of twenty-five, when the prefrontal cortex is developed, we naturally move into our Adult Chair (or at least we do in theory . . . more on that in a minute). The prefrontal cortex is the executive functioning part of the brain able to regulate our emotions (from our Child Chair) and our actions and thoughts (from our Adolescent Chair). It represents our healthy adult self.

This is the self that is able to align with our inner passion and go for it. The self that is aware, lives in the moment, takes responsibility for our life, and makes healthy decisions and choices. This is the part of us that stops blaming ourselves and others for the circumstances of our lives, takes responsibility for where we are, and takes action to step into the life we desire.

When living here, we live more in the present moment than not. We feel empowered and strong, and we feel and process our emotions. When our needs aren't met, we speak up for ourselves and ask for what we want and need. We set healthy boundaries. We know and feel our worth and our value. We know who we are.

Sound like you? Maybe somewhat? A little or not at all?

There is a caveat to living in our Adult Chair: It doesn't just magically happen when we turn twenty-five. There are some "ifs" that determine if we easily slide into our Adult Chair, or if we largely remain emotional adolescents, despite our physical age.

The biggest "if" has everything to do with how we were raised, what was modeled for us, and how well our parents reflected or mirrored for us who we were while growing up. If that was not done well, we are stuck growing up physically as an adult but very much navigating life from our Adolescent Chair most of the time.

I have found over the years that most of us fall somewhere on a spectrum of how often we live in our Adult Chair. Some are almost never in their Adult Chair, and some spend a good amount of time there.

No one spends *all* of their time in their Adult Chair on a daily basis. That would be quite difficult, given that we have an ego that keeps us in the past and future. But that doesn't mean we can't spend a great deal of time there.

If you are not there now, do not worry! You can learn, and it won't take a lifetime! With the right tools, guidance, and your desire to live more freely and maturely, you can live in your Adult Chair on a regular basis!

How the Three Chairs Work Together

The goal isn't for our Child or Adolescent to go away—they are part of us, and they have a job to do! The goal is to get them out of the driver's seat of our lives so we can make wise adult choices, rooted in fact and truth today.

Imagine this: three chairs in a triangle. Your younger self (your Child Chair, or your inner child) sits in one corner of the triangle, your teenage self (your Adolescent) sits in another corner, and at the top of the triangle, there's you in your Adult Chair, the person you are today.

The adult you is reaching for and holding hands with your Child and has a hand on the knee of your Adolescent. Like a loving parent, it listens to and witnesses both of these younger parts, letting them know they are seen and heard but without buying into their stories, survival strategies, or outdated road maps and programs.

In the Adult Chair, we have awareness, and we're able to recognize the voice of our Child or Adolescent, to catch ourselves when we're sliding back into these chairs, and to bring ourselves back to our healthy Adult Chair. Let me share a time I had to recognize I'd moved back into my Adolescent Chair so that I could bring myself back to the Adult Chair.

My son Graham graduated from college in May 2020, during the COVID-19 pandemic, and decided to head to England and attend Warwick University in Coventry for grad school. He had applied to numerous universities abroad, applied for student loans, and was organizing the next two years of his life all on his own (much to my astonishment). During the process, he spent hours researching schools and areas and looking at Google Maps of where he would live, since he couldn't travel there.

I was proud of his focus on the next steps of his life . . . and also, maybe just a bit, struggling to let go as a mom. I often popped my head into his room to check in on what he was doing and what he had discovered during his research.

When I checked in with him on his plans, I found myself swinging back and forth between being a present, active listener, genuinely interested in his findings, to offering my unwanted advice on what he should consider and do.

Graham put his hand up (in a loving way, as I'd taught him to do) and said, "Mom, thank you, but I've got this."

I smiled and said to myself, "Oops, I fell into my fix-it codependency part," then stood up to walk away.

That was me shifting from my Adult to my Adolescent and back to my Adult. I went from the present moment listening with curiosity (Adult) to "fixing" and offering unwanted advice from my Adolescent. (I must also say Graham did a great job setting boundaries from his own Adult Chair. . . . Yep, it can be hard to let our babies be the healthy adults they are sometimes!)

This is how this model looks. We move from experience to

experience, chair to chair, throughout the day, with the goal of returning to and staying in our Adult Chair as much as possible.

The Adult Chair in Action

Charlene came in for a session to help overcome her grief. Her husband had had an affair with his co-worker and left her for the woman he had an affair with . . . five years ago.

She came in blistering mad and hurt. In between her tears and rage, she shared the pain she carried. She would scream about how much he'd hurt her and say she was in so much sadness and grief that she would never be able to overcome it.

I could see that Charlene was keeping her grief and sadness present and was not able to move on from them because she was living from her Adolescent Chair. Her ego mind was focused and stuck in the past, replaying what her husband had done to her and the family. It's not that her feelings were wrong or that her story was not painful, by any means. It was that her ego was keeping her focused on the past and creating perpetual suffering.

In the meantime, her ex-husband had gone on to marry the woman he'd had an affair with and had a child. Her then-teenagers had all gone to college and were out of the house. It was time for her to step into the next chapter of her story as well.

I introduced the chairs to Charlene, lining the three chairs up and demonstrating that her Child was in pain and her

Adolescent was trying to fix it and stop the pain, but it was keeping her stuck by focusing on the past.

I asked her to start by sitting in the Adolescent Chair and sharing how she felt about her ex-husband and what had happened. As she yelled and cried, I let her express her emotions, and I listened with presence. I wanted her to get it all out—one last time.

When she was done, I invited her to do a round of deep breaths and stand up and shake off the old, stuck energy that she was in. I stood up with her and had her mirror my "shake-off dance," and together we spun around, shook, and brushed off the energy of that release. We also did some forceful exhales, saying, "HAAAAA!"

Letting this energy go is important, but even more important is to let it out while being witnessed without judgment or suggestions for improvement or being asked to "calm down." Charlene needed to get it out one more time for us to move on.

I then asked Charlene to move into the chair representing her Adult Chair, and we did a few rounds of deep breaths to slow her down and settle her into that chair. I then asked her to list with me what was 100 percent fact in this very moment: not five years ago, not her opinion or perception, but solid fact in the moment.

After a moment, she stated these facts:

1. My husband ruined our family.
2. My children were devastated.
3. I felt completely blindsided and crushed when I found out about the affair and then the baby.

4. I lost many friends throughout the divorce.
5. My husband was the love of my life, and I thought I was his.

I then asked her to move into her Child Chair and take a deep breath and settle in. "Close your eyes and sink into this younger part of you, Charlene." I recited her five truths back to her slowly. I then asked, "What emotions are coming up?"

"I am devastated . . . absolutely devastated," she whispered.

"What comes up when you feel into 'devastated'?" I asked. "Let yourself fully go into it."

Charlene immediately went into childhood memories of her father dying when she was only thirteen. She began to cry. "We were so alone when Daddy died. He was in a horrible car accident and died at the scene. We were blindsided, and my mother lost her way after my father died. I had to raise myself for the next few years. It was truly devastating."

I asked her what she needed. Immediately she said, "I need a hug. My mother rarely hugged me after my father died. I felt like I had to tend to her, and no one took care of my needs or my grief."

"Would you like a hug now, Charlene?" I asked.

"I would love one, Michelle," she said through tears.

I stood up and gave her a big hug. She continued to cry, then sat down and looked exhausted, but she also had an awareness about something. I asked her to share what was coming up now, from her Adult Chair, the seat of awareness.

"I didn't realize that devastation was the root of all of this.

I knew I had grief with my husband, but it feels as though I have been masking a lot of it with anger. It feels as though the anger was suspending me from fully feeling into my grief. If I felt the grief from my husband leaving, it would overwhelm me, because the grief I still had from my father was in there too. Maybe I was subconsciously protecting myself on some level by not allowing myself to fully go into my grief."

"These awarenesses are excellent, Charlene. They all feel like honest truths for you." I asked how she felt now. She said she felt lighter and even hopeful for the first time in years, as if something had cleared from her.

I then asked her to tell me about her current family, today, all facts from her Adult Chair. She said:

1. My three children are all in college.
2. I moved to a new home and have wonderful neighbors.
3. I have some new friends whom I love.
4. I work out at a gym and have been talking to a man there whom I would honestly consider dating.
5. I started gardening and never knew how much I would love to grow my own vegetables.
6. I started doing yoga two years ago and want to get certified as a teacher.
7. I love to decorate, and my friends and kids say I am really good at it.

I then asked her to move into the Child Chair and to allow any emotions or bodily sensations to become present as I read her the second list. Afterward, she smiled and said, "Yes, that feels really nice." I could see her entire body settle and a look of peace and empowerment wash over her. She had found her Adult Chair. It was easier for her to access this chair having moved through some of the old grief from her father's passing. Now her energy and emotions could move through her body and not feel so stuck.

She was quiet for a few moments, taking it all in. "But my husband . . ." she began.

I stopped her quickly, saying, "Pause and move over to the chair representing your Adolescent Chair, and notice how you feel."

She did so and reported feeling her heart start to race and her body getting tight.

"Yes!" I yelled. "This is the difference between living from your Adult Chair versus your Adolescent Chair. From our Adult Chair, we have choices over what we think about and what we focus on. After five years, everyone has moved on but you. Now that you have touched the core grief and begun to process it, you are going to have to choose to stay in this moment over and over again, which will reroute your neural pathways. You are wired to stay in the past, in blame mode. It's time to rewire and get you in the moment. When you hear yourself say, 'But,' or 'Yeah, but,' that's an indicator that you are moving back into your Adolescent Chair. You can blame your husband for the rest of your life, but it will not hurt him; it is only hurting you and keeping you stuck in anger or grief or other negative emotions. It's all about choice and deciding what chair you want to live in. It's your choice and only yours. You can liberate and free yourself from the past when you move into your Adult Chair. No one has to know but you."

That day, Charlene decided to live more from her Adult Chair. It was not easy in the beginning because she was in the habit of letting her Adolescent/ego mind run her life, but that day she took the reins, learned how to feel and process her emotions, and chose to stay in the moment—and her whole life was about to change.

How to Live (*Mostly*) in Your Adult Chair

To live full-time in our Adult Chair is nearly impossible because of our ego. The goal instead is to live *mostly* from our Adult Chair, as much as we can throughout the day. If you are reading along and realizing that you live in your Adolescent Chair most of the time, it's okay! Take a breath. You can learn this! Anyone can learn to move into and spend more time in their Adult Chair.

The way we do this is first to learn the qualities of each chair. When we learn these qualities, we can catch ourselves if we are not in the Adult Chair. Notice I did not say judge, blame, and shame ourselves. Remember, being human is hard, and we are all doing the best we can.

The rest of this book will be filled with practical advice and tools to help you learn how to get in—and stay in—your Adult Chair as much as possible. Here are the first steps to take:

Step One: Learn the Qualities of the Chairs

The first step is to learn what life looks like in your Adult Chair. You can't choose something you don't know about or understand. Here are the qualities that mark a person in the Adult Chair:

- Lives in the present moment
- Has a raised self-awareness
- Lives with fact and truth
- Observes thoughts (instead of buying into them or taking them all in as truth)
- Busts the stories and assumptions from the ego mind (I call it being a "story buster"!)
- Has compassion for self and others
- Gets curious about what they are feeling, thinking, and experiencing
- Has choices and considers them carefully
- Responds rather than reacts to life
- Feels valuable and worthy
- Sets boundaries
- Witnesses the ego mind
- Can let go and move on
- Owns and takes responsibility for their life and mistakes
- Works with triggers when they arise
- Apologizes when necessary
- Is connected to their inner child and feels and processes emotions

It's also important to learn the qualities of the Child Chair and the Adolescent Chair, so you can notice when you've slid into those chairs that represent the younger parts of yourself. You can find those qualities listed starting on page 23 of chapter 1 and starting on page 73 of chapter 2.

Step Two: Raise Your Awareness About Which Chair You're In

Once you know the qualities of each chair, you'll begin to notice where you are making your choices from and can choose again. Awareness of which chair you are in is the first step.

For example, are you feeling all kinds of emotions bubble up? That means you are in your Child Chair, and your inner child is having emotions.

What are you doing with those emotions? If you're shoving them down or numbing them, you might be in your Adolescent Chair.

With raised awareness, you will start to notice things that you might not have noticed before. It may feel as though someone has turned on the lights in a dark room. Your world will begin to look different. You might notice being around certain people drains your energy, or that a situation at work doesn't feel right in your body. You'll become more connected to your inner navigation system, which might have been numbed out in the past. And with more information, you have more choices.

With time and practice, I promise you will be able to see which chair you're in at each moment of your life . . . and that alone is life-changing!

Step Three: Reach for Your Healthy Adult

When we are not in our Adult Chair, we reach for it. We remember the qualities of a healthy adult and we choose to go there, even when our Adolescent Chair ego wants to pull us in another direction.

We choose the Adult Chair. We can even call it in.

Our Adult is our higher self that comes into our human form. When we live from here, we have a higher awareness of life and what we are going through. We gain new perspectives that we can't see from the limited scope of our Adolescent Chair.

The way to gain access to our Adult is to slow down, regulate ourselves, and call in that part of us. Ask for that energy to enter and wait.

Here are some ways that we can access our Adult when we feel out of alignment, stuck in our Adolescent Chair, or just disconnected:

1. **Ask for your Adult to come in!**
   Simply state out loud, "I need my Adult." The Adult Chair is an energy that we all can bring in. It's the energy of our higher self that will come in and align with us and help us to navigate tricky situations.

2. **Go for a walk in nature.**

   The energy of nature vibrates in the heart. Nature will help us to find our heart and our Adult Chair perspective when we feel stuck or lost.

3. **Journal.**

   Journaling helps us to gain access to our soul. Let the words flow on the paper without judgment. You will find an energy comes through to guide you when journaling. This is your Adult!

4. **Practice mindfulness.**

   Look around you. What do you see, hear, feel, smell, and taste? This is a wonderful practice that brings you into the moment. It brings you out of the ego mind and into present awareness.

5. **Practice gratitude.**

   Gratitude expands the muscle of the heart. Spend five minutes a day thinking of what you are grateful for, then drop your awareness into your heart and *feel* what you are grateful for. This helps blaze the path to the heart and expands your awareness and connection with your soul guidance.

6. **Ask yourself, "What feels right in my heart in this moment?"**

   Living in our Adult Chair means we are living from our heart space and allowing it to navigate us through life. The more you practice living from your heart space, the more aligned you are with your soul. It's about bringing your energy "chin down" and into the body versus "chin up," which is the ego mind of the

Adolescent Chair. Many times, the ego mind has a thought, but the heart has a different idea. Trust your heart! You can't get it wrong.

7. **Get in touch with the part of you that is blocking you from connecting with your healthy Adult.**

   Your inner critic, inner perfectionist, people pleaser, the part of you that feels unloved, etc., might rise up and simply want your attention. When we can't connect with our Adult, acknowledging the part of us that is blocking us from our Adult and having a conversation with it can transform that part and create a pathway and space for our Adult to enter.

Two Practices for Living in Your Adult Chair

Living in our Adult Chair is not something we can typically maintain continually. We move in and out of our chairs throughout the day. Here are two practices that I have found helpful as I strive daily to live from this place as much as possible.

1. Live with Intention

One way to accomplish living in our Adult Chair is by living with intention. The more I lean into the teachings of this model, the more my life slows down, my nervous system regulates, my life seems to get easier, and I live with more peace. But it wasn't always this way for me.

For much of my life, I was busy: I managed my family, maintained our home and yard, grew my private practice into a full-time practice, had parties, and was involved with my kids' sports and volunteering. I was praised by many for how much I could get done.

It may sound impressive, but I was running myself ragged and was driven by my Adolescent Chair. Living with a "go-go-go" mindset takes its toll on the body. On the inside, my nervous system was dysregulated, and I was anxious all the time—and the crazy thing is that I didn't know it! It felt normal to me. My friends would say, "I can't get over all that you can get done in a day, you really 'bust it out,' Michelle." I didn't know any other way!

A part of me felt proud of how much I could get done, but I found that my daily napping and lack of energy were becoming greater and greater. I was ready for bed at eight P.M. and literally could not push myself any longer.

I went to my naturopathic doctor, and she ran all kinds of tests on me. She said that I was unconsciously driving myself so hard that my cortisol levels had bottomed out. I was in stage four adrenal fatigue, and I had massive candida overgrowth! That was the moment when I realized things had to change and change in a big way. I was forty-two years old and felt like I was eighty!

My life changed when I implemented intention into my life. With some help from Wayne Dyer's book *The Power of Intention,* here's how I did it.

The first thing I did was to get very intentional about how I spent my day. I looked for moments where I could change my pace and rewire my overactive nervous system. I decided to not touch my phone until nine A.M., and replaced my morning routine—jumping right into work and activating my nervous system—with morning stillness. This included a morning meditation for ten minutes (at least), journaling, gratitude, and grounding/earthing. Afterward, I took a morning power walk to burn that excess cortisol. Throughout the day, I began to insert "micro-moments" of peace. These are one-minute moments of pausing and either looking out at nature, doing deep breathing, or sitting in gratitude. These micro-moments serve as mini reset moments throughout the day.

Because I was slowing down, I began to notice all of the emotions that were inside of me. I intentionally got curious about them and felt them. This didn't make me "too emotional." In fact, it made me more grounded and solid in who I was. Decisions became easier for me. Boundaries were more obvious in terms of when I needed them and even what to say. I also incorporated deeper inner child work and began an intentional practice of connecting with my inner child daily, even if it was just for a few minutes.

Along with feeling my emotions, I got curious about my triggers and emotional reactions and intentionally sat with both of them to learn from them. Because of this practice and intention, I quickly discovered my childhood emotional wounding. It was incredibly healing and began to transform my life in ways I couldn't believe. I felt stronger and more empowered, and my thinking was clearer. I was feeling deeper self-love and acceptance.

I also started to ask myself daily how my choices felt to me. I tuned in to my heart and let it expand or contract. When my heart would open, I moved toward my choices, and when my heart would contract, I knew that was my higher self/soul guiding me away from that decision.

My relationships thinned out, and the ones that were left were a perfect match for who I was—not a lot of drinking (if any), friends who enjoyed personal work, deep conversationalists, and friends that felt like family. My husband and I faced and worked on issues that I had never noticed before, because I had been moving too fast.

My adrenal fatigue and daily napping dramatically improved. My nervous system became more regulated. I also noticed that my on-and-off depression was a thing of the past. Now when I experienced anxiety, I saw it as an indicator that I was in some way out of balance and needed to center and ground, and it would fade.

It was such a new state of being for me! As I reflect back, I realize what a game changer these simple practices were for me. As much as these helped me physically, they also helped me emotionally, mentally, and spiritually! I found myself settling into my Adult Chair more and more throughout each day.

Intentionality is an important part of living in your Adult Chair. With it, you'll find that when you put yourself first and strive to live in your Adult Chair, your life too will change in unimaginable ways!

EXERCISE

Spend some time in quiet (outside, if you can) without your phone. Go for a walk or just find a quiet space to sit and be with yourself. Bring a journal and jot down your answers if it feels right for you.

1. As you reflect upon your life, what are some things that need to change so you can slow down and reside more in the present moment?

2. How do you distract yourself from the moment?

3. Are you willing to get curious about your emotions? Would you set a daily intention to do this?

4. What is at least one daily practice that you can add to your day that would help you to slow down and enter into the moment?

5. What are you willing to intend for yourself daily to help you to slow down and spend more time in your Adult Chair? Remember, the more time you spend there, the more you see the benefits throughout your whole life. There is an energy to the Adult Chair that begins to permeate all areas of your life and improve the way you live. What are you willing to intend to change your life?

2. Notice Your Triggers

We all get triggered; it's human nature! When triggered, we can be quick to get angry, defend ourselves, and blame others. The question is, what do *you* do when you are triggered? Do you default into drama, or do you repair and clean up the situation? It's not always easy, but healthy adults choose to explore the trigger and do the work around it.

Triggers are a gateway into unrecognized, unconscious beliefs that we have about ourselves. The belief is buried deep in our unconscious mind, but with curiosity about the trigger and some digging, we can connect with our inner emotion or belief and release it!

One of my clients, Carrie, was speaking with her sister, Susan, who asked if Carrie could help out a bit more with their ailing mother.

Carrie turned to Susan and said, "Are you accusing me of not doing enough? I am at her assisted living facility once a week, I pay her bills, and I do more than Greg"—their brother—"has ever done!" Then she spun around and stormed out of the house, slamming the door.

Carrie was triggered by her sister's request, which threw her into her Adolescent Chair and caused an angry, defensive reaction toward Susan. She got in her car and drove off, furious at Susan for accusing her of not doing enough. As she drove home, she realized she was triggered and in her Adolescent Chair. Her trigger was an indicator that she needed to get into another chair—her Adult Chair.

She took some slow, deep breaths and got curious about this trigger. She sank into what she was feeling inside her body and realized that under the anger, she felt judged, and under that, she felt not good enough. This was a familiar feeling that she had felt while growing up. She allowed herself to feel it again now and processed the emotion through.

She then reached for a list of facts (what we do from our Adult Chair):

1. She had been triggered by Susan's question.
2. She had cut Susan off with her anger and never heard the rest of what she was saying.
3. Susan's question had thrown her into an old wound.
4. She needed to repair with her sister.

Carrie picked up her phone and called Susan. She owned her reality by first apologizing for getting upset and storming off and slamming the door when she left. She then let Susan know how she had felt (judged and not good enough) when Susan had asked her that question and reiterated (in a calm voice) that she felt that she did do a lot for their mother and wanted to know what else was needed.

Every part of these steps represents a healthy adult: owning her reality, apologizing (without defending or an excuse), and lastly, sharing her truth to her sister about how it made her feel.

Susan let Carrie know that she appreciated her apology, and that she also recognized how much Carrie had been doing for their mother. She shared that their mother needed to start going for more doctor's appointments due to a new diagnosis. What Susan was asking was if Carrie could help out by taking her mother every other week to these doctor's appointments.

Carrie realized that she had been so triggered that she had cut off Susan's request, and in the end, it was not at all how she had heard it. Now that she understood the actual request, she realized it was something she was able to help out with.

This is a classic example of how life happens. We misunderstand people, get triggered, shut down, get angry, etc. We also very quickly make up stories and assumptions that are not even true from our Adolescent Chair.

How we respond, get curious, and repair is the most important thing after triggers happen. Showing up like both Carrie and Susan did, from their Adult Chairs, is the healthiest way to do this.

EXERCISE

Think of the last time you were triggered. Close your eyes and sink into your body. Bring your awareness down below your chin and notice what might be happening within your body.

Do you notice any tightness or tension? Stay very curious and explore any sensations.

Once you land on something, ask yourself, "What am I feeling?" If the only thing you feel is a physical sensation, this is fine. Keep your awareness on that feeling and watch what it does.

If you notice an emotion, allow yourself to fully feel it. Then ask yourself, with curiosity, "What's under this emotion?" Go with the first thing that comes to you.

Keep going under each emotion until you feel as though you have hit bottom or the root. Then allow yourself to feel that. You may experience emotions or beliefs like "I am not good enough," "I don't matter," "I am not lovable," and so on.

Feel these emotions until they fade. Do not make up a story around one of your beliefs or try to figure out why you have it. Be in it.

Lastly, ask yourself what's true now. Is that old belief still true or not? Are you able to let the belief go? Simply sinking into the truth quite often releases the wrong belief.

The key takeaway here is to pay attention to daily triggers. They are an incredible entryway into healing deeper and hidden beliefs. Don't let the opportunity pass you by.

⁓

Living life from your Adult Chair is simply living from the present moment with raised awareness. If we begin to notice that we are not in our Adult Chair, we do whatever we can to get ourselves there.

With time, the Adult Chair way of living starts to become more and more second nature. Noticing which chair you're in and reaching for tools to help you navigate life's challenges just becomes part of your daily practice.

As my Adult Chair coaches tell me, "This model is not just something you use in client sessions. You live this model; it becomes who you are and how you show up in the world." To live this model is to transform and live a healthier life from your truest, most authentic self.

The Adult Chair portion of this book has been about explaining to you who you are and how you got this way. It's not your fault. It's nobody's fault. The good news—or the great news, I should say—is that there's a way out. There's a way back to yourself, your true self. There's a way into your Adult Chair. All of these things can be turned around. We just have to reprogram. And that is where the pillars come in.

In the upcoming chapters, you will learn the five pillars and tools for living in your Adult Chair. The pillars are the "how" of our transformation into our Adult Chair. The pillars consist of five strategies that we practice daily that will help us begin to raise our awareness and notice when we are showing up in the world from our Child or Adolescent Chairs, and give us the opportunity to "slide one chair over," choosing to act, respond, and live from our Adult Chair.

The pillars are guides and processes to help you to raise your awareness about how you are showing up in the world, shed the parts of you that are unhealthy or limit you, and build a solid healthy adult self: an adult who lives authentically, goes after what they want in life, finds a career that is a match for their heart's desires and passions, and cultivates healthy relationships. Take it slow and steady, and get ready to grow yourself into that healthy, authentic adult!

PART 2

The Five Pillars

*N*ow that you've identified what your programming is from your Child Chair, and what coping mechanisms you developed and still act out of from your Adolescent Chair, you're wondering how to actually make the shift more regularly into your Adult Chair. That's what this next section is all about.

When I thought about what the tangible, achievable hallmarks of being an emotionally healthy adult were, the five pillars were born. These are the core skills that I have learned on my journey of healing, and the tools that I have witnessed over all of my years in private practice that were the most transformational for my clients.

They are the fundamental building blocks of living in your healthiest adult self. Learning and applying each of these pillars will change your life. The pillars are:

1. I Own My Reality
2. I Practice Self-Compassion
3. I Feel My Emotions
4. I Own My Triggers
5. I Set Healthy Boundaries

The pillars build upon one another, with each one giving you the tools you need to take on the next pillar, so start with the first one and move through them in order. At the end of *each pillar, I've provided a hands-on process to begin practicing and applying the pillar in your life. These are simple enough to begin applying today, but they are also skills you can take and use for the rest of your life.*

Buckle in, my friend! Your life is about to shift and change for the better. I am with you on your journey, cheering you on as you move further and deeper into your Adult Chair.

CHAPTER FOUR

Pillar One: I Own My Reality

Rasha came into my office and sat down. "Something is wrong, and I don't know what to do about it."

I tilted my head and said, "Okay . . . tell me more."

Rasha looked down and said, "I can only tell you this, Michelle—and it's really hard to say out loud—I am drinking too much. I reach for wine every night, and it's getting excessive. I can't stop at one to two glasses anymore. I am finishing a bottle every night, and I know I need to stop before I go into two bottles."

I asked her if she had shared this with anyone else, and she responded, "Not only have I not told anyone else, but this is the first time I have admitted it to myself. I have covered this up for too long, and I need to come clean."

I asked her how she felt after sharing that with me.

"I actually feel lighter for some reason, and I am not sure why."

"It's because you are owning your reality, Rasha," I said. "It's the first step to change."

∼

When there's something in our life we don't like—whether it's something painful, something we feel ashamed of, or something we're afraid we'll be judged for—our tendency is to avoid, deflect, or defend.

There are a host of problems with this strategy, but the main one is that *we cannot change what we don't first own.*

That's why the first pillar of living in your Adult Chair is to own your reality.

Owning your reality means taking a good, long, and hard look at who you are today—your circumstances, your choices, your character, and even your family, your past, and your childhood—and accepting it.

It means we take off our masks and our blinders and look at what we might not want to see. To own your reality is to claim who you are, who you were, how you were raised, and how you show up in life.

It's claiming yourself as the person you are today—fully claiming that person, even if you don't know this person, don't like this person, or hate this person.

It's where we start the process of growing into our healthy adult selves.

This step is one of the most freeing steps of all. It sets the stage for the rest of the pillars and leads to freedom, empowerment, and clarity about your life so you can live on purpose with greater peace and love for yourself and others.

We begin here.

Why We Don't Own Our Reality

If change comes from owning our reality, why don't we do it more? I've found it often comes down to three reasons. One, it's painful. Two, we follow our parents' example. And three, our society teaches us it's safer to go along with the group.

Humans are wired to avoid pain and discomfort, physical and emotional, at all costs. And getting radically honest with ourselves could be painful. It might bring up shame, embarrassment, or blame of self for the way we are living or have lived our lives.

It can be painful to admit that our anger issues ended a relationship or alienated people that we cared about.

It can be painful to own that we drank too much, worked too much, had an affair, or made a big mistake as a parent, a partner, a friend, or even a sibling.

It can be painful to think that we carried a grudge or blame for years, and then the person passes away without a conversation, which can cause us to turn on ourselves and create a host of negative feelings.

It's much easier to project on others and say, "They made me do it," but the truth is, we are always responsible for our own actions and how we show up in the world. To own this is to begin our healing and transformation.

The second reason we often struggle with being responsible for our actions is that we follow what we saw modeled by our parents.

Did your parents apologize to each other when there was an issue? Did they apologize to you when they made a mistake or yelled at you because of their own overwhelm?

Did your parents claim what was true without blame or judgment, or did they carry around anger or blame from their own childhoods?

Were one or both of your parents liars who created chaos to distract from what was true?

Everything that happens in our childhood home and how our parents handle life is a model for us. If they blamed, defended, carried anger around, or didn't take responsibility, we inadvertently learn to do the same thing.

And finally, there's a social component to why we don't own our reality: We're afraid that if we're honest with others, we might get kicked out of our tribe, whether that be our friend group, partnership, marriage, family, or community.

This is a primal response. We are innately wired to bond, belong, and be part of a group. If not, it could mean our death. To get kicked out of our tribe thousands of years ago would mean that we would be eaten by wild animals.

The part of our brain that strives to keep us in our tribe is hundreds of thousands of years old, and unlike other parts of our brain, this part has not been updated. This "old" brain pushes us to avoid getting radically honest with ourselves and others to help us survive.

How does this translate into our society today? We become and morph into whoever we feel our group wants us to be. We step into our false selves with others to stay connected and accepted by our tribe. We certainly don't own our stuff.

We think this will keep us safe. But the truth is, owning and accepting our present and past reality is what helps us to become empowered and free, and to live our best and most authentic life. And when we don't own our reality, we stay stuck where we are.

Take my client John, for example. He and his wife, Danielle, had been married for eight years. John had what people call a "hair trigger" with anger. He had no patience and would fly off the handle unexpectedly.

Danielle felt it was affecting their marriage, so she insisted they go to counseling together. When they came in to meet with me, she said she felt as if she had to walk on eggshells around John, and living this way was giving her anxiety from the fear of his unpredictable "flare-ups."

John said that Danielle was overly sensitive. He said it was her issue because she came from a quiet household and just wasn't used to loud voices. He would tell her, "This is how Italians communicate. I'm not angry, and it's not personal!"

Being Italian myself, I understood how expressive Italian households can be. I in no way wanted to put something on John that wasn't true for him, but I also wanted to give him the chance to own this if it was part of who he was. Besides, regardless of who was "right" in this situation, the reality was that it was affecting his marriage, and at the very least, there would be power in owning that.

I invited John in for a solo session a week later to go a bit deeper with him. He sat down and said, "I am telling you, Michelle, this is all Danielle. I am not the problem here; she needs thicker skin."

I asked him if anyone else had ever suggested that he was angry or had a quick temper.

"Yeah, my mother always said that I had a temper, but I believe it's just who I am."

"Did anyone in your family of origin show anger or have 'flare-ups'?"

He said that it was normal to yell in his household; it was just how he grew up. He said his father and grandfather would yell sometimes, but it was not a big deal. He didn't feel anger was something he had learned from his family.

I shifted gears. I wanted him to pay attention to how he was responding in his daily life to those around him, especially how often these "flare-ups" happened. I simply invited him to pay attention to how he was showing up with Danielle, with his kids, and at work. I shared with John the power of owning and accepting our reality, and how it was possible to do this without judgment, blame, or shame. He agreed to try it out.

"I'm going to ask you a question again, and I don't want you to answer it right now. Instead, think about it until the next time we meet." Then I asked, "What if you do have some issues with anger? Could that be true at all?"

John came in two weeks later. He sat down and said, "Well, Michelle, I did what you asked. I paid attention to how often I 'flared up' and realized that it happens more than I thought. My four-year-old daughter runs to her mom when I get upset. I never noticed how often she does that. I also realized that I lose my shit at work more than other people I work with."

John looked down at the floor and said, "I am not sure what to do with this, but seeing how scared my daughter looked really hit me. Until you asked me to pay attention, I didn't notice how much that was happening! What kind of man does this?"

"John," I said, "it's what you learned from your grandfather and your father. It became normalized to you in your home. How were you to know any different?"

John said, "I feel so ashamed of myself."

I was thrilled inside to see that John was tapping into his Child Chair. He was fully connecting with the emotions that were coming up. I knew that fully feeling these emotions would lead him down the pathway of change.

I replied, "Feeling bad is okay. It will help you to shift and not continue this anger in your family. This is the first step to change, John. The next thing to do is to own that you do have angry flare-ups, and it's just like what your father and grandfather did. We do this without blame or judgment for yourself or them. It's simply naming what is and was true. You are doing really big work today."

Inviting John to do this was moving him into his Adult Chair. It was a new "seat" for him, a new energy that I wanted him to experience, one of owning his reality. Sitting here, in his Adult Chair, would begin a cascade of change.

He took a deep breath and said, "Wow, Michelle, this

feels big, but it also feels like without owning this, I can't change it."

I said, "Exactly, John! This is what it's all about! It's not about blaming yourself; it's about learning how to do life in a new way. Without your awareness of this anger, you and your marriage would not only be stuck but heading for a dead end. This marks the day that you and your marriage improve, not to mention the healthy modeling that you will be giving your daughter."

This was the domino effect I was hoping he would realize could happen when he started owning his reality. John and Danielle came in for their sessions the next few months together and had a total transformation in their marriage and family. With his newfound awareness, John learned emotional regulation skills and was able to show up for his family in a new way. Instead of living out of the limiting negative programming learned from his family while he was in his Child Chair, he used this pillar to help him get into his Adult Chair, where he learned how to respond in healthier ways, which created a beautiful cascade of shifts in his family. It started with him but resulted in an improved marriage and greater awareness of his daughter and his role in modeling healthy behavior for her.

The truth is that most of us are doing the best we can with what we were given. Like John, most of us don't want to hurt those we love or show up as less than our best selves. But we all have blind spots, wounds, and programming from childhood that can keep us from doing this. Many times, these wounds even lead to us viewing ourselves as victims, which we will cover in the next section.

By looking at the hard things about our lives, we become empowered to show up for ourselves and others the way we want to—as our most authentic selves.

Getting Out of Victim Mode

One of the identities or personas that comes from our Adolescent Chair is our victim part. Without awareness around it (awareness that we get from our Adult Chair), we might be living from this perspective and not even know it! This is what happened to me.

A common way that we live out of our Adolescent Chair is by believing we are the victim of circumstances or other people's actions. I can hear the "yeah, but" starting now. I understand you may have been hurt by someone in your past—a parent, a friend, a partner—and that pain is real. But continuing to blame them is only keeping you stuck.

I remember one day in my late thirties when I was with my cousin and my sister and I started offering advice (aka "fixing"), without anyone asking for my help (again). My cousin said, "You are so cute with that codependency, Michelle. Don't ever heal that. What would we do without you helping everyone?" She giggled, clearly teasing me.

My response was the same as it had been for years since I discovered that codependency ran through my veins like blood: "Well, if it weren't for Mom leaning on me, treating me like a best friend rather than a daughter, and disclosing so much when I was at such an early age . . ."

My sister jumped in. "Oh yes, we know, Michelle . . . and Dad never had healthy boundaries, and Uncle Don was emotionally abusive, and blah blah blah. When are you going to drop that story? We have heard it a hundred times." The words were honest, and she said them lovingly.

To this day, I still remember where I was standing when she said that. It was as if someone shook me and woke me up out of a dream that was stuck on repeat. It was truly one of those light bulb moments.

I was a therapist. I'd been doing work on myself for years, including working on my codependency. I had even owned it, acknowledging that I struggled with codependency! But I was owning it from a victim perspective! I was stuck in "poor me" and "feel sorry for me."

"If it weren't for Mom and Dad doing this and that, I wouldn't be so codependent. It's their fault!" This was the record playing over and over in my head. It felt good to tell and retell the story of my childhood. I got sympathy, and some part of me liked that.

At that moment, I realized how disempowering that statement was for me. My mother wasn't doing this to me, and my father had passed away years before; no one was keeping me stuck in victim mode but me! I was *choosing* to carry around a story that was keeping me stuck! It was as if I wanted to prove to everyone that my parents messed up, and my codependency was all their fault.

This kind of thinking was not hurting my parents, nor was it limiting them in any way; it was only hurting, limiting, and keeping *me* stuck!

That was the day I stepped out of my victim part and out of my Adolescent Chair. Instead, I chose to take responsibility for how I was living and the story I was telling myself and others. I had to choose to "drop the cement suitcase," as I fondly called it. Carrying that childhood story and blame around was heavy! I decided never to tell that story again, and instead to commit to raising my awareness in my life and becoming mindful of what I was saying to myself and others. When I owned that I was living out of my victim self, that was the day I decided to slide into my Adult Chair and release the story that was holding me in my victim mindset!

The goal of our victim is to get energy and emotional feedback from others. It doesn't know any other way to get love, acknowledgment, or connection. It's an unconscious, adolescent strategy that keeps us stuck in the past.

Once I chose to let it go, it felt as if I had been set free. Nothing was holding me back from becoming the strong, empowered, independent woman with boundaries that I wanted to be. And that is exactly what happened. Now that I'm in my fifties, I continue to become more and more of that healthier version of myself. And it feels amazing!

How can you break free from this victim mindset in your life? You guessed it—by owning your reality!

If your boss continually does not acknowledge your hard work and overlooks you for a raise, instead of complaining about how unfair he is, shift your mindset and action to taking responsibility. Schedule a meeting to talk to your boss about your concerns and ask why you are getting passed over. This means staying out of your victim about why, and instead seeking truth and change for yourself. This is what we would do from our Adult Chair. We notice the drama we want to step into by telling friends and family what a jerk our boss is, but instead we own what's happening and create empowered change for ourselves. Then, after gaining clarity on why you are getting passed over, you get to decide if you stay or go.

Owning your reality does not mean that it is your fault if you experienced abuse or dysfunction, and it does not mean that you are responsible for how you were raised or for others' actions. But it does mean that as the person you are today, from this date forward, you take responsibility for what you do next.

It means stepping into your power, realizing you have a choice, and telling yourself a more empowered story. It means that if you don't like something about your life now, you can do something about it!

This takes work, my friends. It's not always easy. But, if you want to become free, rediscover your true self, and love yourself, it begins with taking responsibility for your life.

How to Own Your Reality

"I've got something to share with you, and only you, Michelle. You told me your office was a vault, correct?" Sherry asked during her session.

I could see, just looking at her, that she was carrying a big emotional weight on her shoulders. "Yes," I said. "It's a sacred vault—nothing will leave this space."

Sherry took a long, deep breath and closed her eyes as she moved to the edge of the couch. "I am going to say this out loud because it feels important to say it. I am not happy in my marriage, and I have not been happy for many years. I have stayed for my kids, and now that they are older and I am spending more time with my husband, I realize I don't love him—and haven't for a very long time. He is controlling and hard to live with, but I put on a mask and everyone thinks we have a perfect marriage."

There was silence in my office. I let her words settle in. Sherry took some deep breaths. "I feel like I just took a five-hundred-pound baby hippo off my chest! I have been living with this for so long. I avoided my truth like the plague."

I nodded, understanding. "Now, what do I do?" asked Sherry.

"It's up to you," I said. "But congratulations, because you just took the first and biggest step to changing your life."

By owning her reality and claiming what was true for her, Sherry opened up numerous opportunities for moving forward that her ego could not imagine! When we own our reality, we are listening (finally) to our heart and soul and not letting our ego or mind override what is true. This creates an openness to change. And that can bring immediate relief, even if the change takes time.

After our session, Sherry had a conversation with her husband and shared how she felt. He was shocked, but he also said he loved her and wanted to try to make their marriage work. They came in for couple's work, and their marriage changed week by week. Her husband was able to see his control issues and work on them. They began to connect in brand-new ways and formed a new and much healthier relationship, different than they ever could have imagined. Sherry was happy again, all because she owned her reality.

I don't want to just tell you about this process, though. I want to walk you through it. The following process will help you raise your awareness around your reality. There are three steps, and each step will provide an exercise to help you to identify what you might need to own in your life, and how to do it.

Take your time, and get ready to take the first step in your new empowered life! The weight you have been carrying will be gone, and freedom will take its place.

Step One: Get Honest with Yourself— Radically Honest

This is a powerful first step. It can be hard to get so honest with ourselves, as our ego's job is to avoid pain, and admitting some things might bring up pain or discomfort. This is normal—keep going! Freedom lies on the other side.

EXERCISE

Find a quiet place where you won't be disturbed. Sit inside or out; use a journal or pad of paper—the idea is to find a space just for you where you won't be disturbed for about an hour.

Here are some questions to reflect upon or write about as you begin to own your current reality. Remember, no blame or shame here—just radical honesty with yourself.

- How is your life?
- What do you avoid looking at or owning?
- How do you change or who do you become when you are with others? Go through the people in your life and get honest about how you show up.
- Are you happy?
- Do you live with daily peace? Why or why not?
- What are you avoiding saying or doing? If there was no consequence, what would you say or do?
- Are you treated well by your partner, your parents, your kids, your friends, and your family? Be honest. How could it be better?
- Do you like your job?
- Do you feel loved?
- Are you in healthy relationships?
- Do you have any unhealthy relationships?
- How do you numb out? Alcohol, drugs, sex, porn, shopping, drama, food, etc.?
- What do you numb out from?
- Do you take care of yourself?
- Do you set healthy boundaries for yourself?
- Does anyone walk all over you?
- Does anyone treat you badly, poorly, or abusively?
- Are you ill and "dealing with it" alone? Have you told anyone?

- How does it feel to connect deeply with others?
- Do you enjoy physical touch? How does it make you feel?
- How is your sex life and intimacy?
- How do you feel about vulnerability?
- Do you feel your emotions? What do you do with them?
- Are you happy in your relationship with your husband, wife, boyfriend, girlfriend, or partner? Why or why not? How do you feel when you are with them?
- What don't you want to own about your kids? Is there an issue you don't want to admit? This could be how they are doing, or how you have treated them, or how they have been treated that you didn't want to see or own. Now is the time to get honest.
- What in your life do you not want to see that is right in front of you? What might you be avoiding?

Write down the answers to the questions that resonate with you. Some questions may not apply to you, but spend time on the ones that do. Spend as much time on this as you feel necessary. There is no right or wrong amount of time. Go at your own pace, but make sure you are going through these questions with radical honesty.

If other questions arise, add them to your journal and write about them.

This exercise is about admitting to yourself what's true that you have not wanted to own or admit to. This is for no one else but yourself. Now is the time to take in the truth about your life.

Step Two: Get Honest About Your Past

In this step, we will work to uncover the ways our past affects our present. It was not uncommon in my private practice to meet with clients who described their childhoods as "wonderful" or "average," but as they shared their stories, it would become clear to me that there were patterns of abuse or dysfunction.

For example, a client might describe their dad as "tired," "losing patience," or "he drank a little," but as I asked more unwinding questions, I'd learn that Dad had a drinking problem and would get drunk, yell at the kids, and "sometimes" hit Mom, and that my client grew up feeling they had to protect their mother from their father.

On the other end of the spectrum, I would also meet with many clients who grew up in quiet or stable households, but our work together would reveal emotional neglect, people-pleasing, codependency, or other unhelpful patterns modeled. Every family has stuff!

Though it's often painful to acknowledge the truth about our childhood, it is an important step to healing. When your eyes are wide open, you can begin the work to change.

EXERCISE

We will begin by looking at your life, from birth to the person you are today. What don't you want to admit about yourself, your parents, your family, etc.? We will approach this in two parts.

PART I

Using the prompts below, start making a list, or write in paragraph form. Let the words flow through you, without editing. This is an exercise to uncover whatever you have not admitted to, or felt ashamed of, or not wanted to see or own.

Once you begin this process, you may notice an energy that takes over. It's like a river of thought that comes through, and the words will pour out on paper once you open the valve and allow them out.

Here are some prompts for you as you contemplate these things. Allow yourself to get creative.

- I secretly . . .
- I am ashamed of . . .
- I don't want anyone to know . . .
- I fear people would judge me or hate me if they knew that . . .
- I will never be able to move on from . . .
- I hate "X" because . . .
- If "X" hadn't happened, my life would have been amazing and so much better . . .
- If only I / my parents / my family had done "X," I would have turned out so much better . . .
- What did my parents teach me about feeling my emotions?
- What did my parents teach me about being honest?
- What did my parents teach me about my abilities and/or talents?
- I was a bully. I was bullied. I witnessed bullying . . .
- My parents modeled for me . . .

- I would describe my parents' relationship as . . .
- I felt close with my parents when . . .
- I felt distant from my parents because . . .
- My parents were my biggest cheerleaders when I . . .
- My parents were healthy in these ways . . .
- My parents were unhealthy in these ways . . .
- My parents favored me / my siblings, and it made me feel . . .
- If I could change anything about my childhood, it would be . . .

Get it all out. Begin in childhood and go up to your current life. You are telling no one these things. This step is just for you.

Spend time with this list. It may take you an hour or a day or a week or longer. This is something that may bring up emotions or not. Both are perfect. This is a space free of judgment or shame. This is your unique experience of taking a good, hard look at your reality and getting it all out in front of you.

PART 2

When you feel you are at a good stopping point, read through your list. If you feel inclined to do so, you can add, "This is me," or "My life," or another title of your choice, at the top of the page where you are writing.

Read through it and notice what comes up for you. Do you want to deny parts of it, or can you accept it as is? Can you look without blame or shame or judgment?

Ask yourself: "What if it just is?"

This is your story that got you to where you are today. It may be a beautiful, messy story, but you are here now. It's no different from reading a book or watching a movie and being able to accept that the book or movie ended this way. We may not like it, or we may feel sad or angry, but it's over, and we accept that it is what it is.

Acceptance does not have anything to do with liking something or approving it. Acceptance is simply accepting what is and was, knowing we do not have the ability to go back in time and change it . . . but we do have the power to change our futures.

Step Three: Own the Good!

Owning our reality also means owning the good about ourselves!

Something that I have witnessed over and over again is how infrequently we own the good. Most people feel uncomfortable doing this, as if they are putting on a pair of shoes two sizes too small.

How do you feel when someone pays you a compliment? What is your response? Most of us don't respond with a "thank you" but instead with something like "This old thing? I got it at Target ten years ago," or "It was not a big deal; no need to thank me." Sound familiar to you?

I invite you to let in and own the goodness that comes your way!

The next time someone pays you a compliment or lets you know how great you did at something, insert a pause before the knee-jerk reaction to deflect or downplay. Take a breath, turn to the person, and simply say, "Thank you." It may feel awkward at first, but after a while, it won't.

Adding some positive self-talk is a wonderful way to anchor in the good. You can say to yourself, "That meal was fantastic; I am proud of myself."

This is not bragging or something you have to broadcast on social media. It's instead something you do quietly with and for yourself. It is a new daily practice where you are looking and listening for the things that you do well and the good each and every day.

∽

This process will also help to build healthy self-esteem and self-worth . . . which leads to our next pillar and another important step in building self-worth: "I Practice Self-Compassion."

If owning your reality brought up some discomfort, practicing self-compassion will help you work through that discomfort and step into an even healthier, more confident version of yourself.

Are you ready? Let's go!

CHAPTER FIVE

Pillar Two:
I Practice Self-Compassion

——

"I am a loser, Michelle. It's as simple as that," Jessie said as she stared out the window. "People clearly don't like me. I have no friends here. I feel like an alien in this world: odd, broken, and unlovable. You are the only person that seems to like me here, and I wonder if it's because I pay you weekly."

"Jessie, did something happen to bring this on?" I asked. Jessie was a relatively new patient, as she had recently moved to Nashville with her job and was working on establishing herself here.

"I went to the hiking meetup you suggested I try, and although there were a few people that were okay, there was no one that I clicked with. It's clearly me! I can't find friends, and I don't understand why it's so hard. It must be because I am a loser, or something is inherently wrong with me," Jessie said.

Jessie's experience isn't uncommon, and we'll return to her story later in the chapter. When someone does not accept us or is unkind to us, we often think it's because of us. Because of something we did or said, or simply who we are. Our ego comes up with all kinds of ideas as to why this person was unkind: "Something is wrong with me," or "I did something wrong," or "I am too much of this and not enough of that."

Every person has an inner voice. In fact, we don't have just one inner voice but many inner voices that guide, judge, shame, or encourage us each and every day. These inner voices are personas or parts that develop in our younger years and continue to guide us into our adulthood. They are mostly unconscious parts that are unaware of who we are today as adults.

The antidote to these voices is self-compassion.

Self-compassion is not just positive thinking. Think of it like taking on the attitude of a supportive friend to yourself. When we feel that we have done something wrong or made a mistake, or when we feel embarrassed or ashamed, instead of beating ourselves up or going into a hypercritical mode, we turn inward and speak to ourselves with kindness and warmth that is accepting and supportive no matter what we might have done. It's a starting point for change.

This concept is foreign to most of us. Instead of being with our emotions, most humans flee and disconnect from our inner pain and suffering. Many of us want to override the softness and go into beating-up mode for being "so stupid" for the choices we made. Some argue that self-criticism motivates them, but in reality, it does nothing for us.

With self-compassion, we learn to stop the cycle of shame and blame, stay connected with ourselves, and tenderly take care of ourselves, much like a friend would do, or a kind, loving parent would do with a child. How you speak to yourself is essential to your mental health and how you navigate in the world. And it's a key practice to living out of your Adult Chair, which is why we'll explore what self-compassion looks like in the following pages, and end the chapter with a number of exercises you can do to help calm your inner critic and treat yourself with kindness.

Why We Don't Practice Self-Compassion

Like all of the five pillars, our self-compassion mirrors what we saw modeled for us growing up. Remember, our road map is created in our Child Chair. Healthy parents are supportive, forgiving, and kind. They tend to our needs. They are warm and accepting. They guide us rather than direct us. People whose parents treated them like this created a road map for them to become more naturally self-compassionate.

However, if we didn't have parents that knew how to be with their own pain and suffering, how could they teach us? If we grew up with parents who were harsh or neglectful, it could lead to developing a stronger "inner critic" in the Adolescent Chair. This is a loud inner voice that beats up on the self and is unforgiving. This harsh inner voice can lead to anxiety, depression, the inability to create and maintain healthy relationships, and more.

The size and "loudness" of our inner critic has a lot to do with how we were parented when we made mistakes. Were you allowed to make mistakes? Were you allowed to make choices that you wanted while growing up, or did your parents dictate the sport you needed to play, the courses you needed to take, the friends you were to hang out with, and so on? Were you someone who was shamed when you spoke up for what you wanted, or perhaps neglected, where it felt as if no one cared what you did at home or at school?

Think of a child who is twelve years old who comes home from school with a bad grade on a test. Telling them they are lazy and could have done better, and grounding them for the bad grade, not only hurts the child but creates shame that runs deep and impacts their self-worth. Some parents believe this motivates the child, but in truth, the child is left with an imprint of "I'm bad" or some other internal belief that lowers their self-worth.

What works better is not shaming the child but instead being with the child in a compassionate way. Getting curious about the child and their test, asking the child what they could have done differently, and asking them what they need creates safety while moving them in the direction of growth.

This compassionate dialogue is not only helpful in avoiding internal shame for the child, it also plants the seeds for how the child will speak to themselves when they make mistakes in the future.

If this wasn't your experience growing up, the good news is that you can transform your inner critic and begin a practice of self-compassion today.

Self-compassion is a form of re-parenting ourselves. Regardless of how you were raised, instead of reacting from your Adolescent Chair, you can step into your Adult Chair and change your inner dialogue by incorporating the practice of self-compassion into your daily life. You can re-parent yourself, quiet down your inner critic, and walk your way out of anxiety, depression, and low self-worth.

Meet Your Inner Critic

Everyone struggles with a critical inner dialogue from time to time. But it's also true that we have the power to work with these parts and overcome these feelings.

Let's say you grew up feeling bad about something, perhaps being compared to an athletic sibling. It might have made you feel less than, not good enough, or unlovable. These core beliefs get programmed into the unconscious mind when we are in our Child Chair. Living with these beliefs running in the back of our minds feels horrible!

When we continue to age and move into our Adolescent Chair, our inner critic comes online and does its best to protect us from feeling those awful beliefs. It may loudly tell us to stop trying, because we'll never amount to anything anyway. Or it may tell us to get small and not be seen or known, as it's too dangerous and opens us up to judgment.

The ideas that come from our inner critic are based on a very young emotional part of us; in fact, it has an average age of twelve. We don't want to get mad at this inner critic part (or any of our parts), as they are trying desperately to keep us safe and alive and included (remember, everything out of the

Adolescent Chair stems from our ego). Instead, we want to thank that part of us and let it know we've "got it" and are going to make some new choices. We can only say these things and have these awarenesses from our Adult Chair.

When my sons were teenagers, I loved when their friends would come over and hang out at our house. Invariably, I would get into deep conversations with them. They knew what I did for a living and would occasionally come to me for advice or life tips. I loved helping or guiding them in any way I could.

We had one of these conversations the day Josh was over. We were talking about the drug scene in high school. My son and his friends might not have told me everything, but they did tell me a lot. I felt as if I had my finger on the pulse not only of what was going on in high school but specifically with my sons and their friends.

Without judgment, I asked Josh if he got high a lot. He replied, "Not a lot, just the normal amount, unless my 'mean voice' is really active, then it's more."

"Mean voice?" I asked with curiosity.

He said, "Yeah, that mean, awful voice inside my head that comes alive when I make mistakes. It's really hard on me and gets loud . . . a lot." He went on to say that he wasn't sure where it came from, but pot was the only thing that seemed to quiet that voice down.

I asked, "Do you mean the voice of your inner critic?"

He looked at me a bit stunned and asked, "You mean you have a voice like that too?"

The look on his face was pure disbelief. He had been keeping it a secret because he thought he was the only one. I know Josh isn't the only teenager struggling with this, and my hope is that more schools will help equip children and teens to learn how to feel and process their emotions, identify their needs, express them, set boundaries, and learn about the parts of self like the inner critic. I'm working on getting the Adult Chair program into schools for this very reason!

I shared with Josh that we all have "internal voices," otherwise known as parts of self, and everyone has an inner critic part. Some inner critics are very loud and hypercritical, and some are not so loud, but we all have one.

In fact, we all have a collection of parts that make up our whole self. Remember that puzzle with one hundred pieces. You have an inner critic puzzle piece and ninety-nine other pieces, like a perfectionist part, a controlling part, a blaming part, etc. You also have parts that drive you or push you forward. You have a confident part and a kind and gentle part and many others. This collection of parts makes up the whole puzzle of self, of who you are and how you show up in the world.

What you need to learn how to do is to manage or become the leader of these parts—the most dominant, healthy voice of all. We call this your healthy adult voice. This is the one that can soothe the harsh voices, be your inner cheerleader when you feel down, and also course correct and even apologize if you make a mistake.

Many times, we abandon ourselves and let our inner critic have a field day with us. We forget that it's just one part of us and fall into the illusion that it's the only part. This is how our inner critic can drive us to perfectionism and control. If our inner critic is loud and we go into verbal battle with it or shove it down, it can lead to anxiety. And when our inner critic goes nonstop without self-compassion, it can win the internal war, which can lead us into depression.

Instead of shoving down our inner critic or giving it more power than it deserves in our lives, we must learn to listen to, accept, and work with the inner critic through self-compassion.

Self-Compassion in Action Leads to Self-Worth

Let's return to Jessie's story from the beginning of the chapter. After Jessie shared how she was feeling with me, I told her we were going to work to quiet her inner critic and practice self-compassion. "I'd like us to make a list with some facts about your life since you moved to Nashville six months ago. Would that be okay?"

"Sure . . . but I'll need your help with that," she said.

I said, "Of course, let's do this together." I grabbed my clipboard, and Jessie and I came up with her list:

1. I moved here in May 2020.
2. I was transferred here with my job.
3. I moved in the middle of COVID during a lockdown.
4. I left a circle of friends in Cincinnati that I was close with.
5. I didn't want to move.

6. Nashville is a destination for so many people who are moving here. There are countless transplants here, now more than ever.
7. I am a nice person, easy and fun.
8. I enjoy hiking.
9. I lean more toward being an introvert versus an extrovert.
10. It can be hard for anyone moving to a new city when you know no one, but especially hard in the middle of a pandemic when everyone is not allowed to see one another.

I handed Jessie my clipboard and invited her to very slowly read the list, each item one at a time. Jessie grabbed my clipboard and quietly stated each item on the list out loud, one by one. I asked how she felt at the end of the list.

She looked up and said, "I don't feel as horrible now. In fact, I feel like I want to say, 'Wow, Jessie, that was really hard, what you did. Give yourself grace.'"

"Yes! That's self-compassion, Jessie. What would you say to a friend or even someone you didn't know who was beating up on themselves, in light of hearing those facts?"

"Give yourself time," Jessie said. "You had everything going against you when you moved here. You are a really nice person, but the pandemic got in the way. Keep going; you'll find your people out there, but it might take a bit of time."

I said, "This list is a combination of owning your reality and moving into self-compassion. How you speak to yourself and treat yourself is important right now, and at every time of your life. It also is the root of healthy self-worth."

I went on to explain how self-worth is an internal knowing that we are valuable and good enough, just being who we are.

Self-worth often gets confused with self-esteem, which is based on our performance or accomplishments. Self-esteem is based on external factors, whereas self-worth is an internal knowing of self and believing that we are valuable and good enough.

Healthy self-worth is at the core of every part of being a healthy human being. It affects all of our relationships, from personal to professional, our mental health, and our ability to grow and thrive as healthy adults.

Without healthy self-worth, we might let people speak unkindly to us, forget about us, and even abuse us. This is why boundaries and self-worth go hand in hand. If I feel valuable on the inside, I naturally want to take care of myself and set boundaries so that other people will treat me well.

Both self-worth and self-esteem are affected by our ability to speak kindly and be supportive to ourselves.

As self-compassion researcher Kristin Neff writes, "Higher levels of self-compassion are linked to increased feelings of happiness, optimism, curiosity, and connectedness, as well as decreased anxiety, depression, rumination, and fear of failure. While lay people often express the worry that if they are too self-compassionate, they will undermine their motivation or become self-indulgent, this does not appear to be the case. Self-compassion involves the desire for the self's health and well-being, and is associated with greater personal initiative to make needed changes in one's life."

Interestingly, self-compassion not only leads to more internal well-being, but it actually facilitates external change and our ability to grow into the people we want to be.

Neff adds, "Because self-compassionate individuals do not berate themselves when they fail, they are more able to admit mistakes, modify unproductive behaviors, and take on new challenges. In a study of self-compassion in classroom settings, for instance, we found that self-compassion was positively associated with mastery goals for learning and negatively associated with performance goals. Thus, self-compassionate individuals are motivated to learn and grow, but for intrinsic reasons—not because they want to garner social approval."[1]

Implementing a practice of self-compassion can grow self-worth and turn someone's life around for the better. It's an inside job, and you can start today. Let's turn to some practical examples and exercises for how you can start to put this into practice and live out of your Adult Chair.

How to Practice Self-Compassion

Our inner voices can be loud or whisper in the background. Sometimes the inner voices sound like a broken record and repeat how awful you are or how you are no good, unlovable, a fraud, will never be successful, etc. Regardless of whether your inner critic is loud and constantly in your head or whispering on occasion, a practice of self-compassion is something we all need to cultivate.

There are a number of tools you can use to practice self-compassion. I'm including seven below that I have found to be effective. Pick the ones that most resonate with you; you do not have to use these in any particular order or all at once. Together and over time, these serve as a self-compassion process you can reach for again and again.

1. **Decide on the voice you want to hear.**
   When the harsh, critical voice chimes in, whose voice would you like to hear instead?

   You can choose your own voice, the voice of someone who knows and loves you, or even someone you don't know. You can pick a movie star or your kindergarten teacher. Did you have a loving parent, grandparent, or aunt? If you don't have anyone that you personally knew who had a kind, loving, compassionate voice, you can imagine Jesus or Buddha or an angel speaking to you. One of my favorite voices is that of Galadriel from *The Lord of the Rings*. She is the angelic-looking elf woman who is the "lady of the woods," and to me, she represents a powerful force of the divine feminine. She is strong, empowered, and loving. When I pull in my self-compassionate voice, I not only hear her voice, but sometimes I take it a step further and imagine her next to me, speaking to me and my inner negative voice.

   It's important to decide on the voice you want to

hear *before* the negative voice or part begins to chime in and shame you. Choose your voice now so you are ready with a counter compassionate voice when one of your parts gets activated.

2. **Unconditional acceptance.**

When we are in a downward spiral, the last thing we feel is acceptance of who we are. Similar to connecting with a compassionate voice, can you get an image of someone who is or was unconditionally accepting of you? Imagine your grandmother who loved you, your best friend, or your favorite teacher speaking to you with unconditional acceptance. What would they say to you? Unconditional acceptance and love means that no matter what you say or do, they are supportive, warm, and friendly with you.

Imagine your person or voice right now. What would they say to you if they unconditionally accepted you? Spend a few minutes with your eyes closed imagining a conversation with this person. How does it make you feel to hear these words? Practicing this when you are not triggered or in the middle of a negative spiral builds up your self-compassion muscle so you can quickly reach for it when your inner negative voice begins. By practicing it for a few minutes a few times a week, it can become your new go-to when you need to practice self-compassion.

3. **Physical touch.**

Do you enjoy physical touch? Not everyone does, but if you do, tune in to yourself and ask, "What would feel good right now?" Get curious about how a self-hug or a hand on your belly or heart feels. Try it out; it may surprise you!

Supportive touch from others can also make us feel safe and accepted. You may want a hug or a hand on your back from someone else. Ask for this if it resonates with you. Personally, when I am in a negative spiral, I reach for someone to simply sit with me with a hand on my knee, and I ask them to listen to me. For me, someone being with me feels so good. It's my way of taking care of what I need.

What would feel good for you? Only you know, and asking for what you need is a form of self-compassion.

4. **"Stop!"**

If we let our inner negative voice run wild, we can spiral into an "inner critic takeover." Learning to stop ourselves before we're deep in a negative thought pattern is a game changer. When you hear that critical voice come in, you can say out loud or to yourself, "Stop!" The moment the voice begins to creep in, saying "Stop," or "Thank you for your input; now stop it," is a self-loving and self-compassionate way to take command of yourself and that voice.

5. **Move!**

Change your physical state. Sometimes standing up and moving to another room or stepping outside for a change of scenery stops the voice. It helps you to become aware of something new.

Putting on music and singing or dancing also creates a change in your state. Doing jumping jacks, going for a walk, or anything that moves you from where you are to another physical location is a wonderful way to break the inner judgment.

I remember standing in my kitchen making dinner one night for my family. Before I knew it, the voice began, and I felt my body get heavier and heavier as I listened to the critical and shaming voice. As if I had woken up out of a bad dream, I realized what the voice was telling me, and I said out loud, "Stop!" I then walked from the kitchen into the family room. The voice stopped.

6. **Get back to the present moment.**

When we get lost in thought, we become unconscious, and our inner critic might see this as an opportunity to step in for a few words. When we do things on autopilot like showering, driving on the expressway for a distance, or gazing out the window, we go into a "check out" mode. This is when we drop into an unconscious state, and it opens the door for the critic. Mindfulness brings us back into the moment where we can take command again and *choose* what we are saying to ourselves.

To snap yourself into the moment, stop what you are doing and look at a plant or a tree outside. Look across the room at a chair or a table. Change your gaze and notice where you are. Get yourself back in the driver's seat in the moment.

7. **Journal.**

Give the inner critic a platform, and let the voice write in your journal. Let it all out on paper. This can exhaust the voice, as it wants to be heard and known. Let it rip, and then bring it to an end after ten to fifteen minutes. Thank it, close the journal, and walk away. Set your timer so you have an end point for it.

Journaling is a wonderful self-compassionate tool to use to cease the inner negative voice.

The more you practice these methods for self-compassion, the more you will find yourself staying connected to your deeper self, your soul. Self-compassion will become a natural way of life for you. The practice of self-compassion is a pathway to reconnection to yourself.

After redirecting your focus back to yourself and choosing kindness and self-compassion, the next natural progression is to also notice how you feel. Emotions are something all humans feel from birth. Have you ever seen a baby not cry? Our problem is that as we grow older, we learn to disconnect from the beautiful and natural energy flow of our emotions.

The curiosity that we feel with compassion naturally leads us into our emotional body. An incredible source of strength, knowledge, and wisdom exists within our emotions. Get ready to expand your awareness even more as we progress into our next pillar, "I Feel My Emotions."

CHAPTER SIX

Pillar Three:
I Feel My Emotions

"My mother was a wonderful mother, but she didn't 'do' emotions," said Grace. For example, she continued, "In first grade, I came home from school crying because some of the kids were bullying me. I had gotten a new haircut, and it was super short. I was so embarrassed and didn't want to go to school that day," Grace said. "The kids were horrible to me! They called me all kinds of names. I told my mom that the kids were really mean and that I didn't ever want to go back to school.

"Her response was, 'Okay, enough of that. You will go to school tomorrow. You are being ridiculous; your hair looks fine. Now go wash up, and I'll make you a snack, and you can do your homework with me in the kitchen while I make dinner.'

"I can still hear her saying that to me like it was yesterday. I remember feeling like I had no place to go or no one to go to with these feelings inside of me."

"How does this affect you now, as a thirty-eight-year-old woman?" I inquired.

"I learned to keep things tucked away inside. There was no one to go to," said Grace. "I notice that it doesn't affect me as much as it affects my fiancé and our relationship. He tells me that I don't feel or empathize with his feelings. He also tells me that I am too calm all the time, and he doesn't really know what's going on inside of me."

I asked if she agreed. She said, "This is exactly why I am here, Michelle. I need you to help me feel my emotions."

Grace's experience isn't unusual. Countless people (both men and women) have said to me:

"I don't do emotions."

"I don't cry."

"Emotions are weak."

"I can't get caught up in emotions. There is no point to them."

"If I feel my grief and pain, it will never stop, so I am not going to feel any of it."

"Why would I want to feel my pain?"

"What benefits do emotions have anyway? They just get in the way of my happiness."

After hearing these types of responses for years, I came to the conclusion that many people don't feel their emotions well. More often than not, we are not even aware that we are having an emotional response because we have consistently worked to tamp down those feelings.

Our Child within is where our emotions come from. When they begin to rise up and be known, our Adolescent/ego does everything in its power to diminish those emotions.

The ideas for "dealing with our emotions" that come from our Adolescent Chair are the strategies of an average twelve- or thirteen-year-old. Think back to your brilliant ideas when you were twelve years old.

I have vivid memories of reaching for pizza when I was overwhelmed at that age. I remember being at a birthday party with a bunch of new friends and looking at the pizzas that were placed on the table in front of us for dinner. My mouth started to salivate, and I could feel this impulse inside of me to eat an entire pizza.

What I know now is that at an earlier age, there were a lot of feelings of overwhelm in my household and with my extended family every summer. There was a lot of drinking on my dad's side of the family and anger between my uncle and, well . . . everyone. It was very unsettling being this little girl, wide open emotionally and very sensitive to the energies in the room, as an empath. I felt all of it, and it was overwhelming . . . until my grandmother handed me my pasta dinner or pizza, or my Jax (think Cheetos, but in 1975). Carbs were my friend, and without any reason behind it, I used carbs (or food in general) to numb out. It was automatic. I didn't even have to think about it.

But our emotions are part of our human experience. Whether joy or sadness, fear or excitement, or something in between, we are wired to feel emotions. Emotions are part of our "inner navigation system," which can give us important information about our lives if we learn to tune in to them.

So, how did we lose our ability to feel our emotions along the way? Before we jump into answering that, let's start with understanding what our emotions are.

Everything in our universe is made up of energy, and our physical bodies, thoughts, and emotions are energy in motion. Our emotions are energy, and they vibrate on a spectrum. Think of a sliding vibrational scale or a yardstick with love at one end and fear at the other. In between love and fear, you will experience emotions such as shame, resentment, bliss, excitement, joy, and grief. When we choose to feel them, our emotions process and metabolize through our physical body, similar to what happens when we eat food and our body digests it. Emotions are the language of the body.

Think of what it feels like when someone says or does something to you that is unkind, hurtful, or mean. It can feel as if someone threw a smothering blanket on you, like it's difficult to breathe, or there's a heaviness on your chest. The emotions that vibrate lower, like sadness, grief, regret, and overwhelm, feel heavy and dense in our bodies.

Now think about when you feel happy, or in love, or when you experience joy. Your body feels light, and you probably experience an openness. The emotions that vibrate higher, like joy, happiness, and hope, create a lightness or expansiveness in the body.

Feeling emotions is one of the core pillars of living as a healthy adult. Are you ready to reconnect with your inner world and deepen your experience with this important part of your humanity? Let's begin by understanding why we have trouble connecting to and feeling our emotions, then explore how living disconnected from our emotions can lead to anxiety, depression, resentment, reactivity, chaotic or disconnected relationships, and even addiction. And finally, as with the previous pillars, we'll spend the final part of the chapter putting it into practice with tools and exercises that will help you to connect more deeply within yourself by learning how to connect to and allow emotions to flow through you.

Why We Don't Feel Our Emotions

Every baby enters the world able to express their emotions and needs. Babies cry when they are hungry, tired, or uncomfortable. Toddlers say they are thirsty or hungry, and they even fall to the ground upset when they don't get that lollipop thirty minutes before dinner! They know what they want, and they express it!

If we are all naturally wired this way, where do we lose our ability to feel and express emotions? It goes back to what we learned about the world in our Child Chair.

Remember, our adult road map is formed from the ages of zero to six years old in our Child Chair. To figure out what happened with our ability to feel emotions, we must consider what we learned, what we were taught, and what was modeled for us during this time period.

If our parents were never taught how to feel their emotions, it's likely they raised us the same way. We teach what we know. If they didn't learn how to feel and process their emotions, how could they teach you to do it? When you were growing up, your parents might have told you to "toughen up" or tried to "fix" your emotions. Maybe your parents *helped* you numb your emotions with a "treat" like cake or ice cream, or told you to watch something on television to "calm down" and "forget about it."

Maybe your parents got divorced, or one of your parents died, or you experienced another tragedy or trauma when you were young. Without the emotional maturity or support system from the adults in your life to process these traumatic events, you might have disconnected from your emotions to survive.

What were you taught about emotions growing up? Do not beat up on yourself if you are someone who doesn't have great emotional intelligence. You can't possibly know something that you were not taught or modeled.

The other issue we run into with emotions is that even though emotions are meant to flow through the body, for many of us, our emotions are getting "stuck." Why?

Like rivers, emotions are designed to move through our system, and when we are operating out of our Adult Chair, this is how we often experience our emotions. But then our mind gets involved and creates a dam in the flow of the river. Our mind tries to figure out the emotion, makes up a story around why we are feeling the emotion, judges the emotion, goes into analysis around the emotion, tries to get rid of it or even project it on others—all of which stops the flow of the emotion, like a dam in the river. This makes it get stuck and linger in the body. This also leads to ruminating and anxious thoughts as we try to use our mind to make sense of what's going on in our body.

Without the interruption of the mind, emotions move through the body in ninety seconds. Dr. Jill Bolte Taylor, a Harvard neuroanatomist, proved this after she had a massive stroke in 1996, which resulted in the left side of her brain becoming temporarily lost. The left side of the brain is responsible for logic, analysis, and speech, and so Taylor was unable to speak, read, write, or remember parts of her past. She only had a connection with the right side of her brain, where we experience intuition, creativity, and emotions. She was essentially transported back to her Child Chair.

Living exclusively from the right side of her brain, Taylor experienced emotions in a new way, which she shared in her book *My Stroke of Insight:*

> When a person has a reaction to something in their environment, there's a 90-second chemical process that happens in the body; after that, any remaining emotional response is just the person choosing to stay in that emotional loop.
>
> Something happens in the external world, and chemicals are flushed through your body, which puts it on full alert. For those chemicals to totally flush out of the body, it takes less than 90 seconds. This means that for 90 seconds, you can watch the process happening, you can feel it happening, and then you can watch it go away.
>
> After that, if you continue to feel fear, anger, and so on,

you need to look at the thoughts that you're thinking that are re-stimulating the circuitry that is resulting in you having this physiological response over and over again.[1]

Taylor's discovery that emotions move through us and don't linger unless we keep them around by continuing to think about them was a profound breakthrough in understanding how we experience and process our emotions. Learning to feel our emotions is a journey back into the body and into deeper connection with self.

The good news is that now that you know, you have the power to do something about it. With raised awareness, we are able to see things from a new perspective—and most importantly, we realize we have choices on how to move forward and create change in our lives.

If we have the desire and will to feel our emotions, we can do it. In a few pages, you'll find a process for reconnecting with your emotions. This tool will provide you with ways to begin to feel your emotions. Before we get there, though, it's important to fully understand the wide-ranging negative impact that not feeling our emotions has on all aspects of our life.

The Impact of Not Feeling Our Emotions

Earlier in the chapter, we discussed how emotion is energy that moves through our body, and how when we experience an emotion on the fear side of the spectrum, it feels heavy in our body. It's natural to want this heaviness, this bad feeling, to leave. There is a way to learn to sit with and feel our emotions, which we will cover later, but since most of us were not taught this, our natural response is that we do whatever it takes to make them "go away."

What strategy do you turn to when you're feeling stressed or upset? Most people numb themselves through things like staying busy, eating, alcohol, drugs, shopping, scrolling social media, or distracting themselves in some other way. You can ask yourself this question without judgment—remember, this is information that you can use to make a change.

Of course, these strategies don't actually make our emotions go away; they just freeze them from processing through us, which causes them to get stuck or blocked in our bodies, like a log causing a jam in the river.

When we block the flow of emotions, over time, it affects our mental health, our relationships, and even our physical bodies. Let's look at the various ways that blocking our emotions negatively impacts the various parts of our lives.

Shallow Relationships

When we aren't connected with our emotions, we tend to have surface-level conversations with friends and loved ones. Going deeper into the emotional realm opens us up to more vulnerability, authenticity, and deeper connection.

Remember Grace? Her disconnection from her emotions

led her fiancé to feel that she was too calm all the time, too balanced, and emotionless. As we worked together to help her to connect and begin to feel her emotions, the result was remarkable. Her whole life started to change.

"It was as if something came alive within me. I had no idea how out of touch I was with myself," shared Grace.

She began to feel the love her fiancé had for her. She began to notice when she didn't like something that he did, and we worked to help her express this to him.

He was over the moon about this! Ironically, he loved that she was mad at him or even upset. These moments created conversations around repair and their love for each other and actually deepened their relationship!

I continued to work with Grace for more than a year, and her relationships with not only her fiancé but also her friends continued to grow deeper. Feeling her emotions created a whole new life for her.

Lack of Empathy

To have empathy is to connect into another's emotional reality and feel what they are experiencing. We cannot do this if we are disconnected from our emotions. Once we get familiar with our own emotions, we can then extend and feel the emotions of others. When we can go into someone else's grief or sadness or shame and be with them in it (without feeling uncomfortable, triggered, or wanting to fix it), it's a beautiful way of connecting with others.

Emotional Dysregulation

When we have a difficult time staying in control of our emotions, highs and lows tend to rule our lives. This also leads to a tendency to blame others for "making us" act or feel *this* way. This victim mindset that we talked about in chapter 4 often looks like not owning our reality and expecting those around us to act in a certain way so that we will not be emotionally triggered.

Instead of owning where the negative emotion is coming from and taking responsibility for how it makes us act, we can fall into blame and shame and project our anger at others. By slowing down, getting curious, and connecting with our emotions, we can better regulate our emotions by recognizing that they are ours. Grounding and allowing our emotions to flow through us with deep breaths gives us the opportunity to discover what belief or program might be under the emotions. We can then "clean up" these limiting beliefs for ourselves. It becomes an empowering act to feel our emotions, let them flow through, and not explode or project them over others. More on this in the next chapter.

Addiction

When we live in a state of suppressing or numbing our negative emotions, this perpetual effort can lead to the formation of an addiction. The more intense our pain, sadness, grief, and so on (from our Child Chair), the more we reach for ways to push down those feelings. This is a strategy that comes from our Adolescent Chair.

Drugs and alcohol are strategic ways to suppress our pain . . . but they're not the only ones. There are a host of more subtle compulsions like achievement, work, shopping, sleep, and busyness that many of us use to "numb out."

Relationships and love addiction are also ways to suppress our pain, as are choosing to create and live with chronic chaos, drama, or suffering. Anything we use to escape from our pain has the potential to become an addiction and will keep us in a stuck state of blocked unprocessed emotions. By connecting with our emotions, we learn to process and release our pain, shame, grief, hurt, and other difficult emotions that we would normally try to suppress. Once we build the "muscle" to process our emotions, the impulse to reach outside ourselves to numb them becomes less and less. We realize we can handle feeling our emotions, even our difficult ones.

Physical Health

Louise Hay, self-help author of numerous books, speaker, and founder of Hay House Publishing, wrote, "We create every so-called illness in our body. The body, like everything else in life, is a mirror of our inner thoughts and beliefs. Our body is always talking to us; we just need to take the time to listen. Every cell within our body responds to every single thought we think and every word we speak."[2]

If the emotional block or stress is left unattended for a very long time, it can contribute to major diseases in the physical body, like cancer, autoimmune diseases, and heart disease, as well as issues like pain in the body (back, neck, etc.), migraines, chronic fatigue, and more. In the endnotes you will find a link to a list taken from Hay's book *You Can Heal Your Life,* which catalogs nearly all of the physical health problems that can have an emotional root.[3]

It's not because our physical body is weak; in fact, our body does everything it can to stay in balance. But when it gets overridden with energy blockages, physical issues occur. So learning how to access and express our emotions can actually make us physically healthier as well!

Mental Health

When the flow of energy is blocked in our bodies, it creates an unsettled feeling that leads to stress and overwhelm, and more often than not contributes to anxiety, depression, low self-worth, and low self-esteem.

Anxiety quite often stems from when we are in our Adolescent Chair and our ego is "pushing" against emotions and trying to "fix" them from our Child Chair or inner child. Imagine two cars facing each other, bumper to bumper. When the drivers hit the gas, the cars push against each other, going back and forth with great force. That is similar to the force that we feel inside of us with anxiety.

The Child is feeling emotions, and as they rise up through

us, the ego from our Adolescent pushes against them. The Adolescent doesn't know how to feel the emotions but can feel the disruption in the physical body and tries to "fix" it by pushing the emotion down or away. This pushing is what creates friction in the body and what we call "anxiety."

From the lens of the Adult Chair, we define anxiety as *the physical manifestation of unfelt emotions.* We also know that our childhood (wounding) or even adverse adult experiences can leave us stuck in fight-or-flight mode, which creates a "hot" nervous system stuck in overdrive. Once we can calm the nervous system and bring it into balanced regulation, we then discover the emotions that might be trapped within, which caused the system to get revved up.

When we get quiet, sit, breathe, feel, and allow the emotions to move through us, our anxiety may decrease. The same goes for depression. Depression can be caused in part by the "depressing" of our emotions. These emotions become buried. By getting curious and allowing the free flow of our emotions through us, our energy begins to move again, and our depression may begin to change.

The Benefits of Feeling Our Emotions

Lisa came in and plunked down on my couch. "I need your help," she said. "I don't like my job, I am not in a relationship even though I want to be, and I'm not sure I like the house I am in."

"Sounds like you have a lot going on, Lisa! That's a lot of dissatisfaction," I said.

"Yeah, I know. I just don't know what to do instead. I feel really stuck."

My intuition guided me immediately to her emotions. I knew the part of her that held the key to unlock all of these changes was in her Child Chair. I knew her emotions would guide her if she could let them flow and get in touch with them.

"How do you feel about emotions, Lisa? Are you in touch with yours?"

"What emotions?" she said with a laugh. "I don't really do emotions."

"How about I reframe that for you, Lisa?" I suggested. "You don't know what to do with emotions, so therefore, you don't do emotions."

"Yep, that's about right. My parents were both chronic drinkers. I guess you could call them alcoholics. They were not mean, or loud, or argumentative, but they drank their problems away. Emotions were not noticed in our home, let alone felt or talked about."

"Well, what if I told you that they are the key to your decisions, to helping you point yourself in the right direction for your future? They are exactly what you need to 'do' in order to find your passion in your job, a new romance, and even your next home!"

"Well, my initial thought is that I want to get up and walk out of here, Michelle," she joked. "But honestly, if they really hold all of this magic as you say, I am willing to give it a go."

Lisa and I began slowly, first working to get her energy in her body. She was very much living from her Adolescent Chair and in her head, what I call "chin up." This is understandable when we don't have parents who model or show us how to "do," or feel, our emotions. If there is not curiosity from our caregivers about what is going on inside of us, we naturally turn off or turn away from our emotions.

Lisa and I did a lot of work around grounding her energy in the moment and noticing what was coming up for her. We began with what she was noticing arise physically in her body. A knot in her stomach, fluttering in her heart, and tightness in her throat were the first physical sensations. Even if we can't name the emotion, the physical sensation and connecting to it is all we actually need!

The next step is to stay connected to the physical sensation until it dissipates (and it always does!). What we are working with is energy in the body. That's all emotions are, and they want to move! We have to stop numbing them, and instead pay attention to them and give them the space to move, metabolize, and flush through us. This takes sitting presently and noticing them.

After a month of weekly sessions and practicing at home in between, Lisa was making *great* progress!

"This is the craziest thing, Michelle. I keep having thoughts and memories of when I was younger and putting together activities when all my cousins would come visit us. We would get together every Fourth of July week in the Adirondack Mountains, and I was the ringleader. I had so much fun and planned activities like kickball, face painting, and so much more. I looked forward to it every year! I hadn't thought about those times in over twenty-five years! For some reason, the memories keep flooding back in."

"Not crazy at all, Lisa! This is what happens when you open up to your emotions. There is an energy that you are allowing to flow through you like a river, when it was previously dammed up. When you allow yourself to feel your emotions, the energy starts to move, your heart center gets activated, and you begin to feel connected to something bigger than yourself. It's a powerful thing you are doing!"

"I had no idea, Michelle! I am having feelings and thoughts of working with kids in some way. I've started looking into it already. There are some schools in Florida that offer this kind of thing with after-school activities and camps all summer. It's lighting me up! It's as though the answers to my questions are flowing into me."

"Yep, this is how it works, Lisa. There is huge power in tapping into our emotions and letting them flow. Keep up the great work!"

At the end of our third month, Lisa had accepted a job in Florida and was moving there to start what she called her dream job. She never knew a job like it even existed. She was thrilled and planned to start online dating when she arrived. She said her whole outlook on life had changed. She felt like a new person.

This is the power of our emotions. And there are numerous benefits to feeling your emotions. Let's go over a few below, then move into some exercises to help you do so.

1. **Our emotions help us to understand and build our sense of self.**

   Our emotions drive us toward or away from ideas, beliefs, morals, and values that do or do not resonate with us. They help build our identity! The more we feel and experience our likes and dislikes, the deeper we know ourselves.

2. **Our emotions lead us to our passion.**

   Pay attention to what lights you up—what activities or thoughts stir up emotions inside. Notice what opens your heart. What excites you? What are you longing for or want more of? What stirs up curiosity for you? Tuning in to what's going on inside of us emotionally will lead us to discovering more not only about our pain and joy but also our passion and what we are here to do and become. Follow your enthusiasm if you want to live a life with passion.

3. **Our emotions guide us intuitively, helping us make decisions and increase motivation.**

   Our emotions serve as a navigation system. When we listen, follow, and feel the wisdom from our emotions, we have the ability to line up with our soul's path. By tuning in to our body and our heart specifically, we can ask a question and feel our way to the answer. If your heart opens and pulls you forward, then you are motivated to move forward with your decision. If your heart closes and your body contracts, the answer is "not yet" or "no."

4. **Our emotions alert us when danger is present and guide us away.**

   When we are connected with how we feel, our emotions can guide us away from danger. The more connected we are, the more accurate our BS meter. You'll be able to feel when someone is going to deceive you, lie to you, or steer you in the wrong direction.

Regardless of how low you are on the "feeling your emotions" scale, you can start today to change that. In the next section, you will find ways to begin to connect with and allow your emotions to move through you.

How to Feel Your Emotions

Our ultimate goal is to be living out of our Adult Chair on a more regular basis. In practice, this looks like being aware of our emotions and letting them move through us in healthy ways. Below are six methods that I have found work really well to help people start to connect with their emotions again. Though they can be powerful when used together, think of these as individual tools you can reach for whenever you need them.

You might find different ones resonate with you at different times. For example, if I'm feeling anxious or overwhelmed, sometimes simply connecting to my body or taking some deep breaths can be enough to move those emotions through me. Other times, sitting down with a journal might be what I need to express and process complex feelings and emotions.

Try these out and see what helps!

1. Get Curious

When you feel an emotion arise, instead of having a knee-jerk reaction to ignore, suppress, or distract yourself from it, pause and get curious about what you are feeling. The next time someone does something nice for you or you watch a feel-good movie, get curious about what you are feeling inside. Are you feeling warm? Comforted? Happy? Content? Appreciative? Something else? Stay curious and allow that feeling to move through you. You may know what the emotion is and be able to name it, or it may be a slight (or large) sensation within your body. You may feel tension, tightness, or a lightness and your heart open. Regardless of what you are feeling, stay with it. It will pass through you like water moving in a stream. Our goal is to simply be with it while it passes through.

Likewise, when someone does or says something not nice, feel this as well. Let the emotions move through you, breathe them through, and don't let them linger with your thoughts. The way we avoid the lingering is to avoid an inner dialogue around the emotion. We don't need to know why we are feeling this particular emotion. We just are. Feel it and let it flow through you.

Many of us are so used to being numb when emotions are present that it can take some work to begin to pay attention and name what we are feeling. What matters most is that today, right now, you have the desire to feel yours. And the easiest way to begin this process is to get curious about what might be inside of you.

2. Drop Below the Chin

If you are someone who does not feel most of your emotions, you more than likely spend all or most of your time in your head (many if not most people live like this!). This is what I call "living chin up." In order to begin the process of feeling emotions, you have to travel into the body and drop "chin down." We do this with curiosity, and we take it slow.

The next time something happens in your life, something lovely like a sunrise (which would elicit a more positive emotion) or something negative like a friend or family member not inviting you to a party, ignoring you, or treating you poorly, get curious and bring your awareness below your chin. Do a gentle "body scan" from the top of your head to your toes, with the greatest emphasis from your chin to your waist. What do you notice? Do you get a sense of what you are feeling? Happiness, ease, joy, fear, worry? Again, you may feel it as a physical sensation of tightness in your belly that may signal worry, or a lightness in your chest, which might signal happiness. Just stay curious, breathe slowly, and see what comes up for you.

Like the previous exercise, for those who have numbed their emotions for a long time, this can be a really helpful way to begin connecting back to your emotions. It's okay if you don't have language to describe your emotions right away. Just notice the sensations coming up.

3. Your Body Speaks!

When you are in the body scan, instead of looking for emotional words, tune in to your body. When you think about an event or what someone said or did, what happens to your body? Does it expand or contract? Do you feel opened or closed? Do you notice a knot in your stomach or tightness in your throat? What happens inside of your body?

When you find the tightness in your body or other sensations, allow your awareness to rest upon that area and breathe. There is nothing to do with it other than be with that sensation. That bodily sensation is due to an emotion that is coming up. You may never know what the emotion is or the name of the emotion, and that is okay; all you need to do is to connect to the body sensation, and the emotion (and body sensation) will move.

As you rest your attention on this part of your body, you will notice that it may start to tighten or loosen. Whatever it does, stay with it! You may also find that it begins to move from one area of your body to another. Just observe it and let it do its thing. This process helps the emotion move through your body, keeping in mind that the emotion is an energy. This energy wants to move and flow, and when you rest your attention on it, it can do so.

If you feel like getting up and moving with the emotion, do it! Tune in to what your body wants to do and how it wants to move. It may be that you dance or stretch or contort your body in a pretzel. It may also be a sound that wants to come out. You may find yourself saying, "Ahhhh," quietly or loudly. Your body knows how to process and release emotions; hand it the reins and let it guide you as to what it needs to do. Your body is wise and wants to be in balance.

4. Journal

When we feel stuck in our heads "chin up" and can't feel our emotions, journaling opens us up to our inner world and gives it a place to be known.

Grab a journal and begin to write. You can write anything at all. You can even start with, "I hate journaling, but I am going to try this today." The key with journaling is to get the flow going with your writing. Once you begin, you'll notice that after a few minutes, words just keep flowing. Do not worry about grammar, punctuation, or sloppiness—just write.

Here are a few journaling starter prompts for you if you don't know where to begin. Use some of these or all of these or use them as a source of inspiration for another way to begin.

- Today I am feeling . . .
- In my body, I am noticing that I feel . . .
- I am worried about . . .
- I am happy about . . .
- The emotion that I might be feeling is . . . because . . .

With journaling, you will find there is more than just what's going on inside of your mind. Journaling will begin to crack you open, and it will help you get to know yourself in new ways. It also helps you to slow down and check in with what's happening inside. I like to say that putting pen to paper gives our internal voices a place to be heard and known.

5. Slow Breathing

It's difficult to feel your emotions when you are moving fast and staying busy. Slowing down and getting curious about what's inside is important. One way to do this is by intentionally slowing down your breath and doing some nice, slow, deep breaths. This helps to connect you more deeply with yourself. You can use this with any of the methods above, even journaling!

Pause what you are doing, sit down, put your feet on the ground, and breathe slowly. Get into the present moment and feel into your body. Allow the emotion to rise up and move through you without meaning or story. Let yourself feel it.

6. Invite Someone to Witness You

You might benefit from speaking with someone else about your experience to help the emotions to bubble up. Here is a healthy way to do this.

Call a trusted friend, family member, therapist, or coach and ask if they are available to talk, whether in person or on the phone. Set up the experience. You can do this by letting them know that you are working through something and would like to share. You set the appropriate boundary for yourself and the experience by setting up how you want it to happen and communicating that to them. You can ask them to listen to you, and, if you need advice, say that you'll ask them for it at the end. You can share that you want them to just hear you out as you vent or emote. You simply are looking to be and feel heard by them. This concept can be difficult for some "fixers" out there, but with clear direction, others can learn how to help you in the healthiest way.

Here's how I do this. When I am upset and need to vent because I can't feel an emotion inside, I'll ask my husband to sit with me and just listen. The boundary I set up is I let him know there is no fixing, talking, or joining in with me around what I am going through or what I am going to share. No matter what I do, I don't want a hug or him sharing how he feels. I need the floor 100 percent and only need to be witnessed. He actually loves the setup because it tells him the best way to meet my needs. Feeling seen and heard is one of the greatest gifts we can give another.

With practice and the intention to feel your emotions,

putting these tools to use regularly will begin to integrate into who you are and how you live your life.

⌒

Congratulations on learning how to feel your emotions! Working and building the muscle of feeling your emotions will alone transform your life in many ways.

Get ready now to move into working with your triggers. Feeling your emotions will set you up beautifully to dive deeper into your limiting beliefs and to heal and transform them!

CHAPTER SEVEN

Pillar Four:
I Own My Triggers

—————————⌁—————————

Stacy came running into my office out of breath. She sat down on my couch and just went off. "I am so freaking pissed at Marissa!"

I asked her what the heck was going on. She said, "I pulled up Facebook in your waiting room just now, and there it was: a post from Marissa that was all about me!"

She explained that they are both members of a private Facebook group for moms. Marissa had posted about something that happened on a playdate a week ago. She said "another mom" didn't discipline her child correctly and that her child bit Marissa's child during a group playdate. She then asked for guidance and opinions from the group on how they would discipline their child if they bit another child.

I said, "Let me guess: Your child bit her child."

Stacy screamed, "Yes! Can you believe that she is putting this out to the public? I apologized and thought it was all done and in the past. It was over!"

Stacy was a mix of tears and anger all at the same time. She was triggered. Sound familiar?

Even if you don't get as hysterical as Stacy was, we all know what getting triggered feels like. It feels awful. We feel like we've been sucker punched in the gut. Getting triggered causes a mixture of physical responses: Our throat may tighten, our body gets tense, we might get a headache, or we may need to run to the bathroom.

Emotionally, we may feel reactively angry and want to throw something through a window, or we may feel simmering anger or hurt or even fall into despair. We feel a range of emotions when we are triggered.

Can you imagine living a life without triggers—or at least fewer of them? Well, you can! Let's break triggers down.

A trigger is a physical and emotional response to one of our own unconscious, unknown limiting beliefs about ourselves. *Ourselves!*

It sounds backward, I know. Most people blame others for triggering them. Many people say things like, "Sammi is so triggering! I can't be around her anymore. She says the most inappropriate things!"

Or: "Jason is such a jerk. He should know what triggers me after all of these years being with him, yet he keeps doing things that piss me off anyway. I think it's intentional."

Or my favorite: "I told my partner/friend/parent/sibling that they need to be more careful and stop triggering me."

But the truth is, when we are triggered, it's *our* stuff! What actually happens psychologically when someone says or does something that triggers us is that the other person is bringing up an unknown, unconscious, negative belief *about ourselves* that is tucked away inside of us.

It's as if the other person is holding up a mirror for us, so we can see, feel, know, and heal an unconscious, unknown belief that doesn't serve us anymore.

The other person doesn't mean to trigger us. They don't do it intentionally . . . and if you know someone who does do or say things to intentionally trigger you, it's still a gift. Every trigger is an opportunity to claim that belief, own it, process it, and transform it, so that you stop getting triggered by that belief!

"Trigger work" is incredibly empowering. You will find yourself living a more balanced life, your relationships will improve, you will feel less stressed and more empowered, and you will develop a healthy relationship with your boundaries.

The best part is that you won't feel victim to others when you have this powerful tool. Simply having the understanding that triggers are ours is in itself part of the transformational journey. Knowing what a trigger is shifts our perspective on them. This is empowering to know.

We'll use this chapter to explore why it is we get triggered, and to learn more about the unconscious mind and how it impacts our lives.

Why We Get Triggered

We get triggered because we live our lives without knowing what our unconscious beliefs are. These unconscious beliefs run 95 percent of how we show up and live our lives. They are responsible for how we act, react, and respond, how we feel about ourselves, our level of self-worth, who we pick in relationships, how worthy we feel, the jobs we choose, the jobs we feel worthy of, how much money we make and don't make, the friends we choose, and so on.

Think of your phone and all of the apps. We are like our phones, and our apps are our beliefs. The difference is, unlike the apps we choose to put on our phones, our beliefs (we can also call them programs) are installed unconsciously.

The unconscious or "programmed" mind is buried under our conscious or "aware" mind. If you think about the analogy of an iceberg, the bigger part of the iceberg is underwater, and the tip of the iceberg is above. This is like our unconscious and conscious minds.

The conscious mind is the part of us that we can see and that we know, but it's a very small part of who we actually are. The unconscious mind is massive and underwater. *These* are the programs that we need to find. These programs or beliefs are running our lives even more than our conscious beliefs. To find these beliefs and transform them is to transform our lives.

As we discussed in the Child Chair chapter, most of our beliefs or programs are "installed" within our unconscious mind by the time we are six years old. We are absorbing everything around us, good and bad, creating programs from what we observe. These beliefs or programs create the road map that we now live our adult lives from. The problem with these programs is that they are recorded by an immature brain without the ability to use discernment.

For example, if a child is in the crib crying for thirty minutes while Mom is on the phone outside, they don't know to say to themselves, "Mommy doesn't know that I am crying because she is outside and can't hear me." Instead, beliefs form like "The world is scary," "I am on my own," "No one cares about me," "I don't matter," or maybe "I am not wanted." Because these beliefs are incredibly painful to feel, we take these shame-based emotions and drop them into the unconscious mind, never to be felt again. Or so we think.

We get triggered because these unknown, outdated beliefs or programs get "activated" again by what someone (or something) outside of us is saying or doing.

One way to uncover these unconscious beliefs is to check in when you feel yourself getting triggered. The next time someone is talking about the opposite of what you believe when it comes to a divisive topic like politics, and you feel lit up and want to argue, take a deep breath and bring your awareness and attention to what you are feeling. You might feel angry (or like the other person is stupid or an idiot). But I invite you to drop below the anger. Make it about you and not the other person. What's under your anger or frustration?

First ask yourself, "How does this conversation or person make me feel?"

The process of dropping beneath your surface feelings might look like this:

Anger: Under my anger toward this person is . . .

Disbelief: Under my disbelief that someone likes that candidate is . . .

Fear: Under my fear that the economy is going to fall apart is . . .

Out of control: The thought of losing everything if the economy collapses makes me feel . . .

Terrified and lonely: When I was a child and my father left, I felt . . .

This is what I love about trigger work. What is discovered under the trigger is rooted in beliefs and memories that we don't consciously have access to in our daily lives. Trigger work reveals and releases beliefs that have been locked away for most of our lives!

Once we discover and feel our core or root beliefs, our lives can then change. We live with more peace and emotional balance. And yes, we get triggered less!

Another way to find your unconscious beliefs is by examining your patterns. For example, do you keep getting fired from your job? Do your relationships keep ending for the same reason? Maybe you keep getting "accidentally" left out of gatherings, parties, or emails from others.

Our beliefs are also *creating* these events as well. These things are not happening to you because you are bad or broken or something is wrong with you. They simply mean that you have some faulty programming.

As an adult, we may feel unlovable unconsciously, so we make unconscious choices to make sure no one will ever realize this about us. This may look like us being extra nice and outgoing with others so that they will never "figure out" or have the thought that we are unlovable. But if we can consciously recognize that we feel unlovable, we can work to change this belief, build up our self-love, and transform how we show up in the world.

You change your patterns by examining your inner unknown (and known) beliefs, just like you would a trigger. We can tackle our unconscious beliefs using the outline at the end of this chapter.

We can change our lives when we know what our programming is.

Bringing Our Unconscious Beliefs into the Light

The question is this: How do we find the programs that drive our behaviors that are buried in the unconscious mind? In a word, our triggers. Triggers are one of the best ways to discover our hidden programs or beliefs.

As humans, we unfortunately do not know when we are living our lives from outdated unconscious beliefs or programming. We tend to blame our circumstances and others for how our lives are turning out. We blame others for our relationships not going well, or jobs we keep losing, or not being able to make money. We also blame ourselves!

But just as with a computer or phone, when we remove

the apps we don't like and add the ones we want, our lives improve. Life gets better.

Trigger work is free, and the process for working with triggers is simple. Doing the work can sometimes feel emotional, but if it changes your life for the better, isn't it worth it?

We can also access these programs in other ways, like hypnosis, journaling, and the "aha" moments in therapy or coaching. These ways may take a bit longer to access, whereas triggers tend to be powerful and immediate.

What I most love about trigger work is we can do it alone with the right guidance. We can certainly do it with another person guiding us, like a therapist or coach, but honestly, we can work the process by ourselves.

This is why I say triggers are a gift. They help us to find unknown programs that are running our lives and work through them. And the more we work with these triggers, the less we are triggered by them!

In my own life, I was triggered often in my teens and twenties. I was emotionally thrown quite a bit. My mood was high and low and angry and sad and happy and balanced. I was all over the place, like a roller coaster. My triggers were ruling my life!

Once I began working with my triggers and discovering these hidden beliefs, I found my mood stabilized. I found myself getting triggered less and less. I share this with you to attest to this work—it's powerful! It's not only powerful but, with the correct guidance, anyone can do it.

You simply need to have the right framework, be brave, and be willing to look at yourself in a deeper and new way.

Transforming triggers is something you can do on your own—anytime, anywhere! Learning how to work with triggers will be one of the most empowering steps you ever take in life.

In the short term, you will learn how to stay in balance even when triggered, mastering the trigger instead of letting it derail your day. You will also find freedom from the unconscious beliefs underneath your triggers. With time, you will find you get triggered less and less. Simply put, the more your unconscious beliefs heal, the fewer triggers you have.

Are you ready to begin this life-changing journey of transforming triggers? Follow the step-by-step trigger process and learn how to work your triggers!

How to Work with a Trigger

Let's go back to Stacy from the beginning of this chapter. She was so upset with her friend Marissa for putting out on Facebook that Stacy's son bit her daughter in a playgroup.

I let Stacy go on and get all of her frustrations out. When she was done, I invited her to close her eyes and take some slow, deep breaths. This is an important step because when we are upset, our energy is moving very fast, and to do trigger work, we need to be able to connect with ourselves. It's fine to get it all out and purge all of our anger and frustration. But then we need to slow down to begin the journey of finding the program/belief in our shadow (unconscious mind).

I asked Stacy to tune in to her body and do a body scan

from the top of her head to her toes and notice any sensations she was feeling. When she got to her chest, she said it felt heavy and like everything was tight and it was even difficult to breathe.

I guided her to slow down even more and get curious about the tightness and go into it with her awareness. She sat for a bit with this tightness and continued to breathe.

I asked her if anything at all was coming to her, and if this tightness reminded her of anything from her past. I encouraged her to let her mind go and wander wherever it wanted, going with the first thing that came up for her.

She sat for a moment and then said that this feeling was oddly familiar. I invited her to take it slow and allow herself to "go there." She then said a memory came up from when she was in first grade. She was in a spelling bee, onstage with her fellow classmates. She was a very good speller but hated being onstage: It made her very nervous and self-conscious. She was one of the final contestants in the spelling bee. It began with her whole class of twenty-five, and it was now down to five kids left on the stage, Stacy being one of them. She said that she was so nervous that it made her stomach ache.

I asked her what was making her so uncomfortable. She said it was that she was onstage in front of others and did not like that feeling.

"What happened next?" I asked.

She said that the announcer called her name for the next word, and she walked up to the microphone. The announcer said the word, and she was so nervous, she peed her pants.

She was mortified and completely embarrassed. The rest of her classmates laughed at her, and she ran off stage and into a costume closet, and hid there and cried.

Tears streamed down her face as she recalled the story and her emotions. I leaned in and let her know I was here with her in this. I then asked if the thirty-four-year-old woman she was today could travel back in time and be with that little girl in the costume closet.

She agreed, and with her eyes closed, I guided her to the closet, and in her mind's eye, she slowly opened the door. I invited her to have a dialogue with this little girl—Little Stacy. I guided Stacy with the words to use with Little Stacy, and here's how the conversation went as Stacy described it to me:

Stacy (S): "Hello, Little Stacy. I have come back in time to visit you. I am you, all grown up, and am a thirty-four-year-old adult now."

Little Stacy (LS): Tears streaming down her face, she turned her head curiously and stared at Stacy.

S: "I am here for you. I am so sorry that this happened to you. I am here for you. Would you breathe with me for a moment?"

I asked Stacy to reach for Little Stacy's hands.

LS: She reached out one hand and let Stacy join hands with her.

S: "How do you feel right now?"

LS: "Like everyone hates me."

This part is key, I said. This could be a core belief from the unconscious mind.

S: "Hmmmm, that must feel bad."
LS: "Yes."

I asked Stacy if she could feel that belief in her body.

S: "My stomach is so tight and nauseous."

I invited her to stay in that feeling, and using her awareness, to just sit in the tightness and nausea and breathe. She did and began to cry again. It was so difficult for her to reexperience this pain. But I knew it was necessary to transform that belief. She sat in it, and I encouraged her to keep breathing.

After a few minutes, Stacy said to me that she hated those kids for doing that to her. I agreed that it was awful and mean. I then asked her if it was true that everyone hated her today in the year that we are currently in. She said no. I invited her to feel into that belief and tell me about what is true instead.

S: "The truth of today is that I have a wonderful husband, my family loves me, and I have some really good friends, and a best friend who would do anything for me."

I invited her to feel in her body what that is like. What was it like to have so many people love her? Could she feel those emotions and physical sensations?

S: "It feels like my chest is opening up and the nausea is going away. There is no more tightness in my body."

Michelle (M): "Wonderful. So, is the statement still true that 'everyone hates me'?"

S: Another deep long sigh. "No, it's not true."

M: "So, what's true instead?"

S: "People love me."

M: "Does anyone in your life now hate you?"

S: "No."

M: "Does Marissa hate you? Take a moment and feel this answer."

S: "No, Marissa does not hate me. She was thrown by my son biting her daughter and wasn't sure how to handle it."

M: "What could be true about her Facebook post then, with her reaching out to others for advice?"

S: "She maybe wants advice on how to handle biting kids and was inquiring to maybe help me with my child, who is a biter."

M: "Could that be true?"

S: "Yes."

M: "Feel that in your body."

After a few minutes, I checked in and asked Stacy what was happening. She said she felt relief and her body was opening. She also shared that she values Marissa's friendship, and, although she felt hurt, she now can see her perspective.

Stacy's energy felt completely different. Her tears had

stopped. She felt solid to me. She now had clarity and a perspective shift on this core belief.

I invited Stacy to connect back with Little Stacy and check in after the process she had just gone through. I asked her to share with her what was true now and to share that she had so many people who loved her. She shared with Little Stacy, and her energy also changed. She reached for Stacy and they embraced.

I invited Stacy to let Little Stacy know what was true: that she was lovable and smart and even safe. I let them connect and share for a few moments, and when Stacy was done, she opened her eyes.

M: "Where else did you see this belief about everyone hating you show up in your life? Let's explore that a bit."

S: "Two ways: avoidance and people-pleasing. I could never figure out why I had this underlying fear or anxiety about people getting mad at me and why I wanted to avoid it at all costs. So I would overcompensate and be extra nice and do what others wanted to do, despite how I felt. I would avoid conflict or people laughing at me or criticizing me like the plague."

M: "How does that feel now?"

S: "Different, but I'm not sure how."

M: "Let's see how you show up now in life and how life shows up for you differently."

Stacy returned a month later, feeling more in balance and peaceful. She sat down in front of me and reported that so much had changed for her. She had no idea how much that belief had programmed her to avoid so much. It was unconsciously making her avoid necessary conversations and conflict, and it made her bite her tongue and not speak up.

She reported that she had not changed 100 percent, but that things were different. She was beginning to feel more relaxed and comfortable with difficult conversations. In fact, what she used to avoid now felt doable, and she was taking the risk and having the conversations.

She even spoke with Marissa and was able to ask about the Facebook post. Marissa sheepishly said that she was uncomfortable posting it, as she didn't want to hurt Stacy, but she also wanted to understand biting and how to handle it. She even apologized to Stacy if the post hurt her, and said that she should have told her about it before posting.

Stacy also reported having conversations with her husband that she had been avoiding, and said he was receptive to her and even open to listening to her. She was shocked!

I asked her again what was true. She quickly replied, "That I am lovable *and* have many people in my life who love *and* support me." She also said how strange "the old her" felt knowing how she feels now.

I agreed with her. It's like a whole new set of possibilities opens up when we work with a trigger and find that unconscious belief. Our perspective shifts, and it's as if we experience a new world. And we do.

Here's the cool thing about working with triggers: Although it can be helpful to work with a coach or therapist as

Stacy did with me, that's not required. Next, I'll walk you through how you can do it yourself.

How to Own Your Triggers

The bottom line is this: Even with all of our uncomfortable emotions and less-than-ideal reactions, triggers are a gift, because they are an opportunity to heal, *if* we choose to pause and look inside at what is coming up *for* us versus *to* us.

This is why the pillar before this chapter is all about feeling your emotions. Feeling your emotions grants you the ability to slide into this trigger process with greater ease. Feeling your emotions is a key element to working with a trigger.

When we work with a trigger, we begin at the "top," with the obvious emotion we are consciously aware of, then we dig deeper and go "under" that emotion and the next and the next, until we discover the root emotion. The root emotion is where the gold is—this is the unconscious limiting belief or program revealing itself!

The trigger process is a step-by-step script you can use next time you are triggered. Not only will this help you react to triggers more consciously, it will help you heal the limiting beliefs underneath the trigger, so you don't get triggered the same way in the future. What a gift!

You can work through this process in your mind with your eyes closed, or get a journal and write out each step— whichever is better for you!

Allow yourself to be fluid. If you feel intuitively drawn to changing or tweaking a part of this process, go for it! Make this process your own and do whatever you need to do in order to shift and transform that belief. Once you go through the process a few times, it becomes automatic.

Step One: What Happened?

Review the scene in your mind or write it out. Another great way to do this exercise is to connect with your inner child, as we talked about in chapter 1. This is how Stacy and I were able to unlock her triggers, and I will use her story as an example in each step below. What occurred that created your trigger? Did something happen, or did someone say something to you? What happened that caused you to be triggered?

Step Two: Bring Your Awareness to Your Body

What are you experiencing in your body? Example: knots in your stomach, tightness somewhere, racing heartbeat, etc. Go into this feeling and be with it for a bit. Simply drawing your attention to the physical sensation in your body helps to begin the transformation of the trigger belief. Remember, the limiting or negative belief or program is an energy that is lodged in your body. When you bring your awareness and attention to it, the transformation begins.

As you connect with your body and sit with the physical sensations, do you notice any emotions coming up? Get curious and notice what is rising up. Close your eyes to help you go deeper into yourself, and take some slow, deep breaths. This will help you to slow down and get curious about what's happening inside of you and the emotion or belief that is there.

Step Three: Find the Core Emotion Under the Trigger

Once you have slowed down a bit, this question will help you to find an emotion or belief coming up: "When 'X' happened or when 'X' said or did that, it made me feel . . ." Sit with and get curious about the emotion or belief that comes into your mind and awareness. If you need a refresher on getting curious about your emotions, refer back to chapter 6.

Emotions are typically "stacked." You may feel angry, ashamed, or frustrated. This is the top emotion. The angry, rageful emotions are our "defender" emotions. We need to go under them. We do this by getting curious around what could be under our anger. Ask yourself, "Under my 'X' (anger, frustration, rage) is . . ." You might be surprised to know that under your anger and rage are vulnerable emotions.

Continue to drop below each emotion or belief until you feel you have reached a core emotion or belief. Take your time and go with the first thought that comes up for you. Do not think too hard. The awareness of what is below the top emotion will come naturally if you stay curious. You'll know you've hit a core emotion or belief when nothing else comes to your mind. You'll intuitively feel that you have hit the root.

Write down the core emotion or belief.

For example, it might look like: **I am angry.**

Below the anger is: **She made me feel less than.**

Below "I feel less than" is: **I am lonely.**

Below the loneliness is: **I am not wanted.**

When you feel below "I am not wanted," and it feels like nothing, then you know you have reached the bottom, your core belief.

Step Four: Uncover the Root of That Core Belief

Once you find the core emotion or belief, stay connected with it, and with your eyes closed, take a deep breath and allow yourself to drift back in time to when that emotion might have first come up for you. Stay very curious and do not try too hard with this. Ask yourself, "The first time I felt like 'I am not wanted' was . . ." Let your mind drift and flow wherever it wants to go. You may feel surprised with what memory or feeling or even smell comes to you. You may not see anything but instead hear the words of your father telling you something that you interpreted as "you are not wanted." Allow your mind and body (which is where your unconscious mind exists) to reveal to you exactly what you need to know.

If something comes up for you, allow yourself to be in it as if you are watching a movie. If you are more auditory, you may only hear words, and this is fine as well. Allow your awareness to guide you back. Your experience will be perfect.

When you arrive back at the scene, notice what was happening that might have created that core belief. Feel into it. If you see yourself as a child, this is fine—feel into that. In order to transform this belief, we must reexperience it first.

If you experience a younger you, be with that younger, vulnerable part as the adult you are today. Sit with them and let them know you are there to listen and are not going anywhere. You can add whatever feels right.

The sky is the limit for what may come up for you and what may be revealed. As unique as each human being is, that is how unique this experience will be for you.

Once you experience the core belief and how it might have been created within you, move to the next step. Know that you may not have any recollection of where the belief came from, and you may only have a sense or a feeling of tremendous sadness when you were young without a specific memory. This is fine! Go with whatever comes up for you.

Step Five: Find Your Present Moment Truth

Think about your life today. Is the core belief that you have identified still true? Ask yourself, "Is this belief 100 percent true, 100 percent of the time in my life today?" Even if it seems true 99 percent of the time, search for the 1 percent and go there. Search for evidence that it is not.

It might be only one instance. For example, if my core belief is "I am not wanted," ask yourself, "Is this 100 percent true today? Does anyone in my life make me feel wanted?" You can even think of people who might not be in your life any longer, like an ex-partner or grandparent. Did they want you? Does your boss want you around? Does your dog or cat want you? Stretch your mind and find the opposite belief from "I am not wanted."

This is important, and you'll need to do this part, even when you don't want to and even if it feels as if you are letting someone "off the hook." This is for you and for your reality to change.

Step Six: Choose a New Belief

Your old core belief might be "I feel ignored," but after questioning it, you conclude that it is not 100 percent true 100 percent of the time—your best friend lets you pick where you go to lunch and respects your boundaries.

Now ask yourself, "What else could be true?" For example, "If my best friend lets me pick where we go to lunch and respects my boundaries, then what else might be true about other people?" You must get radically honest and not fight this. "Could it be true that some people hear and respect me?" Find the new belief that resonates with you.

Step Seven: Own Your New Belief!

State your new belief to yourself out loud and slowly. Close your eyes and feel in your body what happens when you state this belief. For example, "I do matter." "This brings tears to my eyes to hear/feel this." "I feel joy." "My body opens." Get curious about how your body responds to this new belief.

After repeating this new belief to yourself a few times, until it feels solid, bring up your original belief and notice how it feels. Play with the two beliefs and notice how the original belief feels different. This is your chance to choose the new belief and let it land in your body and claim it as your own.

Go back to the previous experience of when you discovered the root belief. You might have felt, sensed, seen, or heard something when that root belief was formed. Maybe you are seeing a younger you on the playground, with siblings or a parent. Perhaps it's just words that you hear. If possible, go into that experience again with your new belief, your new truth, and let the younger you know what's true now, and that the original belief was not true, or is not true any longer. Let yourself feel the new truth in your body (you may feel your body expand as you do this) and breathe in that new belief. This process will anchor it in and shift your past experience.

Open your eyes and take a few long, slow, deep breaths. You are done! Your old limiting belief has now been "updated"—no different from how you update your phone or computer. Claim this new belief for yourself. You can even use it as a new daily affirmation. Put your new belief on your mirror and look at it daily. Claim it!

The most beautiful thing that happens when we do trigger work is that our external reality changes. Changing our outside world and reality is all about us cleaning up our own limiting beliefs. Life and the people in our lives begin to show up differently. It feels like magic, but it works!

∽

You have made it through the first four pillars! This is big work. Once you have begun to put into practice the first four pillars, you probably feel different. You might be showing up differently, or people might be commenting that you are more peaceful or even (I love this one) "Did you do your hair differently?"

What they are feeling is that you are changing for the better! Your self-worth is growing, your sense of self is expanding, and you may already feel that you like yourself better and even are beginning to love yourself a bit more.

Quite naturally, the last pillar is boundaries. Boundaries are not scary when we know what they are and how to use them. Take a moment now to compare your new self to who you were before you began to make the discoveries you have in this book. Doesn't it feel like it's time to protect this new empowered you? We do this with boundaries.

Turn the page and let's dive in.

CHAPTER EIGHT

Pillar Five:
I Set Healthy Boundaries

———————— ༄ ————————

Years ago, my new client, Debbie, arrived at my home office for her ten A.M. appointment and rang the bell. My two-year-old son, Graham, ran to the door and greeted her, sucking his thumb while rubbing his "ducky blanket" on his cheek.

Debbie looked down and said, "Well, hello there!" I appeared then and Graham shyly moved behind my leg to hide from her. My babysitter, Tracy, was late and I was so embarrassed to be meeting a client with my son at my feet. It felt unprofessional.

I had just opened a part-time private practice out of my home a month prior. I searched long and hard to find the perfect babysitter for my son—one who loved kids, who would keep him quiet and entertained while I was with clients, and whom I enjoyed being around too.

I hired Tracy the moment I met her. We clicked right

away, and she felt like family. She *loved* kids, and Graham adored her as well. There was just one problem I discovered in the first weeks of working with her: Tracy was always late.

When I hired her, I let her know the importance of arriving thirty minutes in advance of my first client so we could all get settled in before my workday started. But it turned out that time management wasn't her strength, and she would regularly arrive just in time for me to greet my client, if not later.

A few minutes after I greeted Debbie, I heard a car door slam and saw Tracy jump out, full of apologies. She grabbed Graham. "Go, go," she said. "I know your client is here! I am so sorry!"

Later that afternoon, I called my friend Brooke. She asked about my day, and I vented to her about how embarrassed and angry I was about Tracy being late *again*.

"This is the second time she has been late in two weeks! It's so embarrassing to have my clients here and my sitter not here! I can't leave a two-year-old to fend for himself!" I huffed. "I am over it! I'm going to fire her!"

Brooke asked me what felt like the most obvious question: "Have you told Tracy that you are upset, and that you need her to be on time or else you have to let her go?"

"Well, the day I hired her, I told her she needed to be on time," I said.

Brooke asked, "Have you reminded her of this again since you hired her? Since both you and Graham love her so much, why not give her at least a warning? Maybe she needs to know how much this is affecting you."

I was silent. Her suggestion gave me knots in my stomach. My throat got tight. "Well, that sounds like an uncomfortable conversation."

Brooke laughed and said, "It's called a boundary, and you need to set one, Michelle. She is an incredible person and might just need reminding. Don't give up on her too soon."

Does this sound familiar? Someone in your life is doing something that causes you stress, hurts you, or makes you uncomfortable. But instead of having a conversation, being honest with them, and asking for what you need, you avoid the tough conversation altogether. Meanwhile, anxiety is building, resentment is growing, and the relationship is fracturing.

This is a sure sign that a boundary is needed!

I finally worked up the courage to sit down with Tracy and let her know that arriving late wasn't working for me. Because I shared openly with her, she began to understand how her tardiness was affecting the quality of my sessions. She told me she loved our family and would start leaving ten minutes earlier to be sure she was on time or even early.

Tracy ended up working with me for years, eventually watching my second son, Blake, while my practice grew. I'm so glad I didn't give up on that relationship too early . . . or give up on myself and what I needed!

The fifth pillar of being a healthy adult is setting healthy boundaries. Simply put, a boundary teaches others how we want to be treated. Boundaries are how we protect ourselves, our peace, and our energy. And very often, they're how we protect our relationships.

Think of your identity as your home. You are proud of and love your home. You decorate it to your liking and buy your favorite things for it. You plant trees and flowers on the land around it. Because you love your home, you naturally want to keep it safe, so you put a fence around your property. The fence serves as a boundary that protects what's inside of it: your property and your home.

When we set boundaries in our personal lives, just like building a physical fence around our home and property, we are protecting ourselves, who we are. Our boundaries protect our ideas, beliefs, morals, and values.

This fence isn't about keeping people out (though it can do that). It is about creating a protective barrier between yourself and the outside world to keep you safe—emotionally and physically.

Yes, there are some people whom we cannot be in healthy relationships with (and this is when extra strong boundaries are needed), but many of our relationships can be happier, healthier, and more peaceful through this simple method of communication.

Regardless of your experience or history with boundaries, you can learn now how to set them! In this chapter, you will discover what a boundary is, what it isn't, and how to set healthy boundaries, including boundary scripts. Let's begin our journey into the final pillar.

Why We Don't Set Boundaries

While we know it's important to set boundaries, most of us aren't great at it. Why is that?

Why did it feel so big to me when I thought about setting a boundary with Tracy? Why did I feel physically ill at the idea of sharing my want and need with my babysitter?

The answer comes not only from my own personal journey but also from the thousands of people I have worked with over the years.

The typical response that I heard was that boundaries were uncomfortable. Others felt that boundaries were confrontational. The codependents and people pleasers would have rather died than to speak up for themselves and run the risk of hurting someone's feelings (I was in that group, so I get it!). I will share a story from my client Chloe later in this chapter that exemplifies this attitude perfectly.

The truth is, we don't set boundaries because we are not taught how to do it in a healthy way.

Most of us either lived with parents who were too strict and had extreme or rigid boundaries, so as adults we don't want any boundaries, or we had parents who were non-confrontational and lived life "just letting it go," which affects us as adults in a different way. Other parents wanted to set boundaries, and would get mad and frustrated, but without healthy boundary modeling from their own parents, they didn't know what to say or how to speak up. No judgment here toward our parents. But today we begin to change our programming around boundaries.

Another common reason for not setting boundaries is low self-worth. If you don't feel connected to your sense of worth, then you have nothing to protect! Boundaries aren't even a consideration in that scenario.

So a key element to boundary setting is taking a look at your self-worth. I can hand out boundary statements the length of this book and tell people when and how to use them, but if you don't feel worthy or valuable deep inside, you won't be able to speak them with conviction. But when you believe you're worthy of protection, boundaries will follow.

If you need to, revisit pillar two on self-compassion, which leads to self-worth. See how all of these pillars work together like building blocks?

If you are someone who avoids boundaries, you may not realize that not setting boundaries can create fatigue and exhaustion. It takes a lot of energy to discount ourselves and suppress our needs and our voice.

When we don't set boundaries, we hurt and devalue ourselves. Some of us let others walk all over us and get their way just to keep the peace. This is not healthy and is probably a pattern that was learned in childhood.

Not speaking up for ourselves and allowing others to dictate how we live and how we show up in life can create a loss of self and not knowing who we are. This can produce anxiety, not feeling worthy, a general feeling of apathy, or even depression. I saw this firsthand with my client Chloe.

"What do you mean, stop calling my mother daily . . . that would crush her," said Chloe. "You know how my father is with her; they bicker so much, and my sister of course is of no help. I am the only one she has to listen to her. In fact, she tells me I am her best friend, and she can't imagine us not talking at least once a day."

Chloe was a forty-two-year-old mother of two who was chronically fatigued and drained.

She was there for her mother, her kids, her husband, her friends, and anyone who needed her. In fact, she was there for people even before they knew it. She loved to help people and to be there for them. She was involved with book club, neighborhood Bunco, and volunteering at her kids' school. She also was in charge of welcoming all new neighbors (like a Welcome Wagon) into their neighborhood.

She came in because she was exhausted. And based on what she shared with me, I wondered about people-pleasing and codependency and a severe lack of boundaries.

She prided herself on being a giver and felt like a good person when she did it. She couldn't imagine not showing up for others and giving 110 percent.

My internal codependency alert alarms were going off. I knew the signs all too well:

1. Overly giving of herself to all.
2. Meeting the needs of others before they knew they had needs.
3. "My mom is my best friend," a phrase that sends up a red flag. We can be close and have amazing relationships with our parents, but the "best friend" label always leads me to wonder if Mom is oversharing and

leaning too hard on her daughter. And I was correct in my intuition.

4. Having a full calendar of volunteering and helping everyone.

5. Not spending time alone or doing what it takes to recharge herself.

6. Fatigue or feeling drained.

7. Being horrified at the idea of putting self first, as if it's a foreign concept.

8. Growing up in a drinking, possibly drug-using family with the risk of addiction.

9. One or both parents leaning too heavily emotionally on a child in the home, using them as a confidant, oversharing adult concepts, concerns, anger, etc. with the child.

10. Overall lack of boundaries with others and self. Not being sure where other people end and she begins, tending to "blend boundaries" with others.

11. Rather than feeling her own feelings, guessing or assuming others' emotions are her own. Suppressing her own emotions to avoid pain, discomfort, and suffering.

12. Lacking a strong sense of self to know who she is, not feeling empowered or claiming her own space, instead feeling guilt.

The first thing Chloe and I worked on was gaining clarity on her current reality and owning it. After exploring her history, she realized her mother had leaned too heavily on her since she was a child. She also gained awareness around her overdoing for others that was a main contributor to her daily fatigue and feeling drained.

Then we moved into feeling her emotions. She felt the grief and other emotions of her younger self and the childhood that was lost from her mother leaning on and depending on her during her formative years.

We also worked the muscle of feeling her emotions when she started to erect boundaries first with her kids, then her husband, then others, including her mother.

"I feel so much guilt, Michelle. How can I tell my mother that I can't call her every day anymore? Who will she turn to instead of me?"

When erecting boundaries, guilt can come up when we are programmed to please and help others and disregard our own needs, wants, and desires.

"Feel the guilt, Chloe," I said. I gave her a minute or so to feel into it.

"I can't breathe, Michelle; my whole chest is tight."

"Allow your chest to feel tight and keep feeling the guilt. Let's notice what happens next—just keep breathing."

A few minutes later, she said, "My chest is not tight. . . . I don't feel guilt anymore. . . . I feel sadness now. . . . I am aware of a little me inside that feels really sad that nobody is paying attention to her."

"Perfect, Chloe. Imagine being next to her. Turn toward her from the forty-two-year-old adult self that you are today, and let her know that you are here with her now, and you see her and want to get to know her."

We moved directly into working with her inner child.

We uncovered deep emotional pain, feelings of abandonment, and overwhelm for having to take care of both of her parents and taking on too much.

"Allow yourself to feel all of it." Chloe sat and cried and cried. So much trapped pain was released that day.

As we continued to work together, she learned all of the pillars and was practicing them daily with great results. I could see a new self forming, a stronger, empowered self that she was cultivating as she practiced the pillars. It was organically happening so beautifully! After a few months, she could see a clear shift in her sense of self, in who she was and was becoming. She started to like herself. The more she erected boundaries, the more she created space to get to know herself and realized she liked herself!

Now it's time for you to learn how to stay connected to your new self, set boundaries, and feel the emotions that rise up around your boundaries.

EXERCISE

Before we get into further helping you understand why boundaries are so important, what they look like in action, and how to create your own, let's start by first considering what was modeled for you growing up, with an exercise called Boundary Contemplation. Grab a pen and paper or journal and answer the following questions honestly.

- What did your parents and other family members model and/or reflect to you while you were growing up?
- Was it comfortable or uncomfortable to speak up in your household?
- Was your experience while growing up one where you got shamed, made fun of, laughed at, bullied, or criticized when you spoke up for yourself or shared your ideas or beliefs?
- Were you encouraged to speak up for yourself in your family and share your needs?
- Were you ignored and left alone, and did you have the feeling that no one really cared about your needs, ideas, or beliefs?
- Were you expected to merge with one or both of your parents' needs, ideas, and beliefs and abandon your own? Instead of speaking up, many of us learned to be people pleasers and to take care of others' needs—or worse yet, to anticipate their needs even before they know what their needs are!
  - We might have done this to keep the peace in the household and keep everyone happy. We learned to suppress or detach from our needs and instead put our focus outside ourselves.
  - We also might have learned that speaking up for ourselves to an adult was impolite or even rude and just not allowed. You might have learned that "Good girls/boys don't speak this way."
- On the other hand, others were raised in a home that had a lot of anger, rage, and even violence. Was this your experience? Speaking up for yourself in a home like this could

result in a dangerous outcome, so it was better to protect yourself by staying silent.

If we weren't modeled, taught, or encouraged to speak up for ourselves and share how we feel and what we need, we can't possibly know how to do this now as adults.

As you write down your experience, note that it's not uncommon to have some childhood wounding, trauma, or programming that needs healing before we can get free of patterns like people-pleasing and peacekeeping. Inner child work, as discussed in the Child Chair chapter, is a great place to begin!

Common Misconceptions About Boundaries

Most people do not set boundaries because they have misconceptions about what boundaries are and when and why we use them. It is important to understand how healthy they are, and how vital to living as healthy adults in our Adult Chair.

Let's get clear about what boundaries are and are not by clearing the misconceptions around them.

Misconception One:
Boundaries Are Confrontational

This is a big one. Most people don't like conflict and fear disconnection—and when we don't understand what boundaries are, they can feel like conflict or even feel "mean" and confrontational.

Aiden had been coming to me for a month to work on his relationship with his partner, Jenny. She tended to explode on him and then sweep it under the carpet as if nothing had happened.

In the meantime, he would feel physically and emotionally frozen and thrown by her yelling.

The truth was that Jenny had unresolved issues from her past, and her anger about that was leaking out all over Aiden. She needed a boundary.

Another problem was that Aiden had grown up with a mother who was a rager, and it used to terrify him. The idea of speaking up to Jenny about her anger was triggering him into his past with his mother, and he could not find a way to set a boundary with her. It felt way too scary.

"I don't like confrontation," said Aiden. "I'd rather just let it go and move on with my life."

If I had a dollar for every time I've heard this, I'd have a huge savings account! I let Aiden know that a healthy boundary was not confrontational. A healthy boundary teaches others how we want to be treated, and it's a conversation.

"Your mother's rage was an unhealthy confrontational boundary," I said to Aiden. "Let me teach you another way."

I explained to Aiden that a boundary was simply a way in which we share our reality and our needs with other people. A boundary can be confrontational when done with rage and anger, but it does not have to be. In fact, the healthiest of boundaries are created by speaking your truth directly and being firm and to the point, without yelling or blaming.

This felt new to Aiden, but as I shared with him some boundary scripts and statements (which I will share with you as well), he began to get it.

"You mean I can just tell Jenny it's stressful for me when she yells and ask her to communicate more calmly?" he said.

"Yes, that's all you have to do," I said. "No need to accuse her or blame her, and no need to fight about it. A boundary is just you sharing *your* experience and what *you* need."

Misconception Two:
Boundaries Require an Explanation

Many of us feel we have to justify our boundaries or explain why we have them. For example, instead of saying, "Thank you for the invite but I can't attend your party on Saturday night, I have other plans," you go into a list of explanations as to why you can't attend. Your explanation is so long that the person becomes lost as to whether you can even come to the event or not!

You don't owe someone an explanation for why you are setting a boundary. Simply having a need is enough reason for setting a boundary. And oftentimes, a one-word response is all you need for your boundary. You can say:

- No.
- Stop!

- Don't!
- Enough!

For example, if I run into a friend on a busy street corner and I notice a bicyclist coming by who looks like they may hit them, I may yell, "Look out!" and pull them out of the way. This is a short boundary statement that has a lot of energy in it.

If someone is screaming at me and is out of control, I may say, "Stop!" and walk away. One-word or short boundary statements are fine and work very well.

Misconception Three: Boundaries Must Be Spoken Out Loud

Sometimes boundaries can be silent. These include:

- Hanging up on someone speaking abusively to us.
- Not participating in a conversation when we feel the speaker is being passive-aggressive, rude, spewing anger or rage on us, or gaslighting us.
- Walking out of a room, a meeting, or a home if someone is speaking in a mean or belligerent way.
- Not showing up at an event, party, or holiday function if we know that someone is going to treat us in a bad or inappropriate way or make us feel uncomfortable.

Boundaries are not about changing another person; they're about protecting yourself.

Examples of Healthy Boundaries

Now that you have an understanding of boundary misconceptions, here are some common examples of healthy boundaries.

Example One: Tina

Tina's mother-in-law, Cheryl, was over-the-moon excited about the new baby. She wanted to spend time with her new granddaughter, and she popped over to the house three or four days a week, every week, to "help out." Neither Tina nor her husband had ever asked her to do this.

Cheryl was a sweet and loving person, but Tina needed a break from her and wanted to spend some time alone with her baby.

It was time for a boundary. Here's an example of what Tina could say:

> *"Cheryl, I can't thank you enough for all you have done for us and the baby. I love that you want to spend time with the baby. Can we come up with a schedule for when you come over moving forward? I am craving some one-on-one time with the baby. Let's discuss the days and times for your visits that work for us both."*

The way we present a boundary is key, especially with someone we think may not take it well. People close to us who are not "boundary savvy" can feel hurt when we speak up. Often, expressing gratitude or reinforcing how much you value the relationship before setting a boundary can help disarm them.

Boundaries need to be direct and specific. For example, if Tina had said, "Don't come over so much," it could have sounded to Cheryl like something very different than what Tina had in mind. Defining a schedule moving forward was key to Tina's healthy boundary.

Example Two: Jerry

Jerry was a forty-three-year-old divorced father of two. He had been dating Christina for eight months. Christina was thirty-five with no kids. Jerry was in love with Christina and had been thinking about marriage with her. He also loved his kids and missed them desperately. They were eight and ten, and he only saw them on Wednesday nights and every other weekend.

Jerry introduced Christina to his kids around month three. She was loving and kind with them in the beginning, but he started to sense Christina getting colder toward him and short with his kids on the weekends he had them. Jerry couldn't understand why Christina's posture had shifted.

It was time for him to gather information. Here are a few statements he could use to do that:

"Christina, I love you. You mean the world to me. I have noticed in the last few months, you have started to act dif-

ferently when we are together with my kids on the week-ends. Can you help me understand what is happening so we can work this out together?"

"Christina, I have noticed that you have been very quiet on the weekends when I have my kids. I would love to know what is coming up for you so we can work this out."

"Christina, I have noticed that you are less patient on the weekends when I have my kids. You seem irritated and short. Can we talk about this? You matter so much to me, and I want to help any way I can."

When we seek to understand and come into a conversation with curiosity and an open heart, rather than with our defenses up, ready for battle, it helps the recipient to lower their defenses and stay open with us.

Example Three: Emily and Brad

Emily and Brad had three kids: fourteen-, sixteen-, and seventeen-year-old boys. The boys had less-than-solid boundaries, and their household was getting out of control. Brad believed that the boys needed freedom, as his own parents had been way too controlling. He wanted them to feel supported and loved and have total freedom.

Emily wanted a curfew for them and some house rules.

She came from a strict upbringing, and Brad feared that she was going to be too strict with them, so he had always pushed against her.

Emily and Brad needed to meet in the middle and establish some house rules for the boys. Here are some of the house rules they came up with:

1. Ninth- and tenth-grade curfew will be at eleven P.M.
2. Eleventh- and twelfth-grade curfew will be at twelve A.M.
3. Everyone is responsible for their own dishes. If you eat something, when you are done, put your plates and silverware in the dishwasher.
4. Everyone is responsible for their own laundry.
5. There will be a rotation of clearing the table and doing dishes. Each boy has a night that they are responsible for.
6. Each week, the garbage and recycling is taken out on a rotation.
7. The lawn will be mowed, weed-whacked, and leaf-blown by the boys on a weekly rotation.
8. No drinking or drugs allowed in the house.
* All rotation chores will be on a calendar in the laundry room so everyone knows what they are doing and when. If anyone does not take care of their chores, there will be a consequence. These consequences will vary based on age, from taking away the car for a day or longer, grounding for a day or longer, or taking away electronics for a day or longer, depending on the severity of the violation of the house rules.

The key was that Emily and Brad agreed and came to the boys as a unified front with the new house rules. When it comes to boundaries with kids, unified and clear communication is the most important thing. If kids see their parents are not unified, they will be less likely to respect the boundaries that are set.

How to Set Healthy Boundaries

Healthy boundaries require us to be connected to our emotions. We ultimately *feel* when to set a boundary based on our emotions—something or someone may create a tight feeling in our bodies, or in our heart, or we may feel uncomfortable, unsure, or even unsafe.

Doing the work with our emotions is essential to setting boundaries. They serve as our internal navigation system, and our bodies will dictate when we feel violated. This requires us to drop below our chin and learn how to connect to and stay connected with and grounded in our bodies.

When there, we are connected with our inner world, which represents the inner boundaries we want to protect. When our inner boundary has been "bumped" or violated, we then set an outer boundary. This is when we let the person know what happened and what we need or want instead.

Boundaries and speaking up for oneself can feel scary if we didn't witness how this was done while growing up. We may want to avoid them at all costs. But with boundary guidance, you too can be a boundary badass. It just takes a little training and guidance.

Regardless of where you are on the boundary spectrum, here are the steps to crafting healthy boundaries. You'll notice that it's a lot more than just finding the right words. Boundaries are a full-bodied experience.

1. Know Thyself: Building Internal Boundaries

The very first step in setting boundaries is to get to know yourself—your beliefs, ideas, morals, and values. This is how you know what you are protecting, what matters to you, and what your boundaries are.

No two people will have identical ideas, beliefs, morals, and values. That's what makes each of us interesting and unique. That's why there isn't a right or wrong when it comes to boundaries; they are highly personal.

When our boys were in high school, my husband and I held the belief that nothing good happens after midnight. So we expected our kids to be off the roads after midnight, either at our home or sleeping over at a friend's house.

This was a house rule and something we valued, so we set this boundary with both of them and let them know that if they violated this boundary and came home after midnight, there would be a consequence.

Boundaries help us honor the unique qualities that make up who we are and protect them.

EXERCISE

Carve out some time to come up with a list of your inner beliefs, ideas, values, and morals. These are yours and do not have to please anyone else. Knowing these things within yourself will help you to know when to speak up for yourself.

Once you come up with your list, write it down in your journal, and notice how well you protect your inner boundaries. What could you say or do to set a boundary?

2. Hold Your Energy

Our words carry energy. You have probably had experiences where you thought, "This person has no energy; they seem lifeless to talk to," or "There was no energy in that handshake; it felt weak." We are interpreting energy all day long, and the same is true when we're setting a boundary. If you don't own your boundary and "hold your energy" strong behind it, the other person will be able to feel that you don't really mean it.

But when our words have our energy in them, we are heard *and* it takes fewer words because people feel their impact through the energy that we are expressing.

One way to make sure you are speaking with energy is to speak from your belly and not your throat. Try this right now. Say out loud, "Don't say that to me again," from your throat. Then breathe deeply, and this time speak the same words from your belly. You will be able to feel the difference.

Another way of understanding this is through the concept of power. When we connect to our power, we can express our boundaries, and people hear but more importantly *feel* them.

Holding your energy requires that you get really solid with yourself before you set a boundary with someone else. When we know what we need, what we expect from others, and who we are, we feel energetically embodied and solid. This is our power. We can own who we are, claim who we are, and, yes, protect who we are.

Amber came in exasperated from having yet another dead-end, frustrating conversation with her soon-to-be-ex-husband, Mark.

"He is such a narcissist, Michelle. I do not know how to deal with him! He twists everything I say around, blames me for everything, and quickly explodes into anger over what seems like the most benign thing! How am I supposed to come up with a clear parenting plan with him? He doesn't listen to me or hear a word I say."

I asked Amber to stand up and hold a big red plastic ball in her arms, hugging it tight. I told her this ball represented her power. I told her I was going to be Mark, and she could be herself. I wanted her to practice holding her power.

She began with a typical conversation they would have. "Mark, I need you to please stop giving Katie"—their daughter— "so many sweets on Sundays before you drop her off. She is having a hard time falling asleep with all that sugar."

Responding as Mark, I replied, "What are you talking about? She has no problem sleeping at my house, and we always have dessert after dinner. This is clearly because of how emotionally unstable you are." Then I grabbed the red ball from her arms and pulled it into my arms.

"It was way too easy for me to grab your power," I said. "You deflated and didn't have any energy around the ball!"

She said, "I know! You used words that he uses with me, and I felt my muscles go weak. I couldn't hold the ball!"

I said, "No, your muscles went weak because you couldn't hold your power . . . and it's time you do. With narcissists like him, Amber, you won't win. Your goal is to speak minimally to him, and to stop asking him for help, because he will battle you every time. Your job is to maintain your power. That means no matter what he says, you are going to stay connected to yourself and let his words fly by you like someone is throwing cow poop at you! You duck and let it fly by, and for sure don't let it land! You instead want to maintain your composure, your posture, and your power. Stay connected to what you know that's true. One, you are going through a divorce with him. Two, you have not been happy in years. Three, he is emotionally abusive. Four, he has a lot of unhealed wounding and projects his pain on you. And five, you are looking forward to being done with this divorce and moving on with your life."

Amber said, "Dang, Michelle, when you say those things out loud, you remind me why I am doing all of this. I was so strong to muster up the courage to leave, and now I am faltering when he talks to me. I know this is right for me and us and especially our daughter. I don't want her to witness such an unhealthy relationship as a model for how two people should be together. That I am clear about."

I said, "*Yes,* Amber! How do you feel in your body right now?" Without any hesitation, she said, "Solid and powerful." "Let's grab the ball and start again," I said.

Amber hugged the ball tightly and repeated the same request. I immediately reached for the ball to grab it, but this time, I couldn't! Amber held the ball with stoicism and a calm, grounded, solid energy. I did everything I could but couldn't pry the ball out of her hands!

I asked how she felt, and Amber had a huge smile on her face. "Powerful," she said.

At the end of our session, I gave her a little plastic red ball and told her to take it with her and hold it in her pocket while she was with him or had to read an email from him, to remind herself to hold her power with him. A year later, she came back with her little red ball and said how life-changing the "red power ball exercise" was for her.

When you connect to your power, it makes setting boundaries and letting things go much easier. Connecting to your power helps you to hold your boundaries, not lose yourself, and let go of what is unimportant. Staying connected with yourself and in emotional balance becomes your top priority.

EXERCISE

Do you hold your energy well? Why or why not?

What needs to change for you to hold your energy better?

What can you imagine or say to yourself to strengthen the inner powerful you? Can you use words of self-compassion to strengthen your inner power?

We all have this ability to become powerful. Stand up right now and say out loud: "I am powerful!" Stomp around and state this out loud. "I claim my power!" You have this energy within, so claim it.

3. Stay Out of the Weeds

Another thing to consider when setting a boundary is to "stay out of the weeds." Instead, you should give your answer politely but succinctly.

For example, imagine you invited me to a party Saturday night, and I didn't want to attend. A few days before the party, I bump into you, and you ask me if I am coming. I scramble a little bit and say:

"It's so great to see you! I am sorry I have been out of touch. Did I mention that my son is home from South America? It is so great to be with him even though it's just a short amount of time. We enjoy spending time together every morning and taking long walks. We even started cooking together! It's been so great to spend such quality time with him. This weekend we are actually going up to Asheville, so we won't be around. We are going hiking on Grandfather Mountain then heading up to Boone."

Did you catch the boundary, or was it hard to follow? We often fill our responses with fluff because we feel uncomfortable speaking up for ourselves. A healthier response without weeds sounds like:

"I am sorry I have not replied yet. No, I am not able to come this weekend. I have plans with my son, but thank you for the invite."

This is polite, to the point, and clearly answers the question about attending the party.

Boundary statements with too many words are confusing. The receiver doesn't understand what you are saying when there are too many apologies and explanations. It's a benefit to both you and the person to whom you are responding to answer directly.

EXERCISE

Are you too wordy, or are you direct? Grab your journal and create a boundary statement.

Now, take a look at your statement and see if you can tighten it up even more and take out any extraneous words. Will the person you are speaking to understand it? Is it clear and concise?

4. Set "Bullet Point" Boundaries

The antidote to getting stuck in the weeds? "Bullet point" boundaries.

Bella came into my office and she was furious! Her fiancé, Richey, had bought tickets to a concert for himself and his friends and didn't invite her to go. She was beside herself and even wanted to break off the engagement.

After asking her to take a few deep breaths, I asked, "How did it make you feel when you found out that Richey didn't buy you a concert ticket, in a word or two?" She closed her eyes and got quiet for a minute.

Bella replied, "Abandoned and unloved."

"What do you want moving forward?"

She said, "I want to at least be asked or included in the future."

I said, "Perfect! Now, let's put these truths of yours together in a statement—but in bullet points—for Richey. I am guessing he didn't really hear what you said earlier and probably defended himself."

Bella quietly said, "That sounds about right."

"What you want to share with Richey instead is how you felt and what you want or need in the future." I asked her to try on this list of bullet points and let me know how it felt:

- Richey, when you didn't include me with the concert tickets, it made me feel abandoned and unloved.
- What I would like instead is to be asked or included in the future before you make purchases like this.
- Would this be possible?

Bella agreed that this would be a better approach, and that she'd try it.

See the difference? Bullet point boundaries are powerful because they are direct and to the point, and they convey exactly what you want and need. Setting boundaries in this way feels powerful.

EXERCISE

How clear and direct are you? Is this something you are willing to practice?

Practice this week being very mindful of speaking up for yourself, using fewer words, and being more direct. Think about structuring your requests in just a few bullet points.

5. Use "I" Language Versus "You" Language

When we begin a boundary saying, "*You* did (or didn't do)," the receiver of the boundary moves into a defensive posture and doesn't hear what you are really saying. Using "I" statements about how you feel and what you need will lower the recipient's defenses and help you take full ownership of your boundaries.

Though staying out of the weeds is important, there are some statements we can use to help make the conversation feel gentler and lower others' defenses. When you ask something like "Can you help me to understand . . . ?" it typically takes people out of their defensiveness and opens them up to helping. People like to help if they can. It also puts you in the position of gathering information, rather than assigning blame, which is a more productive place to be.

For example, if you were hurt by someone not returning a phone call, you might say:

"I cherish our relationship and feel very close to you. Can you please help me to understand why you never returned my phone call?"

Not only will this help open the recipient to hearing from you, but it will reinforce how much you value the relationship, and allow you to gather information with curiosity so you can understand what boundaries are truly needed.

EXERCISE

Become mindful of how often you start a sentence with "You" versus "I." This week, develop a practice of slowing down and paying close attention to how you frame your statements.

Set a clear intention to start using the word "I." This is empowering and will help you to strengthen your boundary muscle as well as your "Owning Your Reality" (pillar one) muscle!

6. Create Strong Boundary Statements

Creating boundaries can be as simple as communicating one statement, and I'll even give you an example to fill in below. A boundary statement should contain what happened, how it made you feel, and what you need.

"I felt _____" + "I need/want/prefer _____."

Expressing what you need or want can often be phrased as a request—for example, *"Could you please _____?"*

Here are some examples of strong boundary statements:

- "Laura, when you didn't invite me to the party, it made me feel sad and left out. I need to know if we are still friends." *(Sometimes a boundary might begin with gathering more information.)*
- "Joey, your comment hurt my feelings. Please don't say that to me again."
- "I felt abandoned when you never checked in with me after my surgery. I would feel really cared about if you checked in on me."
- "I felt overwhelmed when everyone at dinner laughed at me and you did not defend me. I need you to stand with me in this relationship and be on my side."
- "I was filled with worry when you didn't call me when you got home. I need you to check in upon your arrival home next time, please."
- "Thank you for the invite. I am unable to come that weekend."
- "Please don't speak to me with that tone; it's making me feel uncomfortable."
- "I asked you not to come without calling first. Please let me know the next time you are heading this way, since it disrupts my workday."

- "Mom, I am not going to be able to call you daily with my new job. I'll call you on Saturdays."
- "Please let me know if you are going to be late next time, so I can shift my schedule too."
- "Please lower your voice. It's making me feel scared."

EXERCISE

Walk through the prompts below, in order, to determine where you might benefit from setting a boundary in your life, and to practice creating your own boundary statements. You might want to use your journal to think through this.

1. Who in your life do you need to set a boundary with? Who is making you upset, uncomfortable, or hurt?

2. How are they making you feel? Sad, hurt, ignored, invisible, unlovable? Tune in to yourself and ask, "How do they or what they are doing/saying make me feel?"

3. What do you prefer? What would be helpful moving forward? What do you need? Remember that a boundary is not about ending the relationship; it's about getting your needs met and coming up with a solution so that this doesn't happen again.

4. Craft your statement and practice it. Are you speaking from your belly or throat? Are you confident in what you are saying? Do you believe you have a right to speak up?

∽つ

Boundaries are not mean; they are self-loving. They are a practice of self-compassion and a sign of self-worth. Many times, they are also loving to the person you are setting the boundary with, giving them clear communication that lets them know how best to show you love and respect.

Once we learn the structure of what a boundary is and what goes into a healthy boundary, we can then practice setting boundaries in our own lives. The more you practice, the easier it becomes. Remember to give yourself grace, as this may be a new concept for you. A baby learning to walk will fall and be wobbly in the beginning, but eventually they walk and even run with ease. The same is true for boundaries.

Setting boundaries gets easier as you practice them. Once you get the hang of them, you'll experience how nonconfrontational they are and instead how empowering and affirming of your worth!

Your Best Future
in Your Adult Chair

———————— ✑ ————————

Throughout these pages, I've worked to give you a road map for how to truly change your life. Now what?

This is where the rubber meets the road. You have a decision to make: to take these concepts, apply them, and incorporate them into your life . . . or to keep on living the way you have been, even if you're not as happy as you could be with your life.

I hope that by now, you are noticing the areas in your life where growth is needed. My friend, growth is always needed! We can always evolve a bit more, grow a bit more, love ourselves a bit more. It takes choosing a path and committing to yourself. My hope is that *this* is your path. The Adult Chair pillars and principles are simple concepts to learn, and with conscious effort, they will change your life, as they have already changed countless others.

It comes down to choice and desire. You first must choose not only this book but the purpose of this entire book.

Its purpose is to help you reconnect to yourself and live a balanced, emotionally healthy, peaceful life with purpose and fulfillment. This is what it means to live in your Adult Chair.

Unfortunately, most of us humans live our lives disconnected from ourselves. Personally and professionally speaking, in the last few years, I have never heard from so many people who feel lost or lonely, or who live with overwhelm, some sort of fear, or anxiety. Many people are on medication just to help them to navigate life.

On the outside, most of us present well and "normal," but on the inside, we might question ourselves, hear the voice of self-doubt, be unsure of who we are, and wonder if we are likable or how we fit in.

Connecting with ourselves, our bodies, and specifically our hearts opens up a world that we did not know existed in human form.

The truth is, the connection that we long for and are searching for outside ourselves is one that we are already connected to; we just forgot this truth. We must remember who we truly are: Source energy in human form.

This energy flows right through us, and once we learn to reconnect to it, we remember—or better yet, we have an experience of—who we truly are, and our lives change in unimaginable ways. We become unstoppable. We live with passion, purpose, and enthusiasm. We live with self-love and stop seeking it outside of ourselves. We realize how powerful we are, live with intention, and become mindful of our thoughts. We work like hell to process and transform our triggers. We learn to process and move emotions through us, because we understand that emotions are energy. They are our built-in navigation system from Source/God that is here to help direct us in life, to live our highest, healthiest life.

I follow a motto that I intend to live with every day, and I invite you to join me in adopting it into your own life:

I will let nothing and no one disconnect me from myself.

This means that no matter what I experience in my outer world, I commit to finding ways and tools to keep me connected to myself, which is my soul, a sliver or aspect of Source/God that is always flowing through me. When anything happens in my life, I ask myself, "Why is this happening *for* me? What can I learn from this experience?" versus "Why did this happen *to* me?" It changes the energy completely and helps me to stay anchored in my Adult Chair. I am 100 percent dedicated to this.

I am devoted to soul alignment. When we devote ourselves to this, we transform our lives.

Let nothing disconnect you from yourself. Make this choice, let these tools help you to stay aligned, and you will have a life in which you are living from your highest self— a life that is passion-filled, one where you experience more joy and laughter, one where you enjoy yourself and others, one where you feel more relaxed, at home, and at peace with yourself.

This is life in the Adult Chair.

Review these tools and begin to apply them to your daily

life. They will become not just something you use but part of how you show up in life. They will transform your life from the inside out.

All you need to have is the will and desire to choose yourself. The time for change is now. I will be with you every step of the way, cheering you on from afar. Sending you so much love.

Gratitude

I sit here deeply humbled and overflowing with gratitude for so many. It's a challenge to summarize all the people I have gratitude for. But I'll do my best.

First and foremost, I extend my heartfelt thanks to all the clients I served over the twenty-five years of my private practice. This book was inspired by the work that I did with all of you! Thank you for your trust and belief in me, even when my methods seemed "different." You took a leap of faith in my unique blend of traditional and holistic healing, and together, we soared. You know who you are, and I love each and every one of you. Thank you.

To the more than ten million listeners of *The Michelle Chalfant Show:* You are the wind beneath my wings. Along with my clients, you made me realize the importance of my message and encouraged me to share more. Thank you for your dedication to personal growth and for following the show. You inspired me to write this book after so many of you asked, "Is there a book on your teachings?" Well, here it is. Thank you.

To my incredible Certified Adult Chair Coaches: I am so grateful to all of you for feeling the call to join our army of light warriors and change the world alongside me! You all felt the pull not only to become Certified Adult Chair Coaches but to bring massive healing into the world. THANK YOU all for your dedication and love for the Adult Chair model and the tsunami of healing you are bringing into the world. I love you all!

To the countless mentors and teachers who have illuminated my path with incredible truths and insights and contributed to my own healing journey and also to this book: You know who you are. Thank you.

To my husband, Graham Chalfant: You are a pillar of unwavering support in my life. You have never doubted me or my abilities and have always been my biggest cheerleader. Thank you for your patience with my work and with this book. When I would say, "I am almost done writing, just one more weekend, that's it!"—inside you knew it would be many more weekends, and you NEVER complained. You are my rock, my steady anchor. From day one, you have embraced who I am fully. You always said that I was not like others, and you loved and accepted me fully. All of my "woo-woo" ways mixed with my obsession for deep personal work—you accepted all of it. You witnessed my path with curiosity and constant support, often joining me in my explorations. Thank you, babe. I love you and am grateful to be with you in this lifetime. It's a good one.

To my sister, Nicole Magryta: my rock, my soul-twin. Where do I begin? You have been my encourager, my steadfast supporter, every step of the way. You have always had my back and would fiercely defend me against any adversity. Thank you for your divine intuition and for brainstorming with me so many business ideas! I can't imagine my life without you. Thank you for listening to my ideas and giving me your honest feedback, always. There's no one quite like you. Thank you, babe.

To my sister/cousin, Cara Maddox: So much I could say here. You have brought the heavenly realm to earth for us, sweet sister. I have always felt a deep soul connection with you that transcends this realm. Your heart is like none other. You are incredibly special to me and a constant reminder that the heart is the way home. You have always been a source of encouragement and grace, not only with this book but in my life. I am so grateful to have you as part of my life (again and again and again). Clearly this is not our first rodeo together and won't be our last. Our connection is like nothing I have known, and I am eternally grateful for your continued love and support always. I love you, sweet sister. Thank you.

To my son Blake Chalfant: Our morning check-ins have been the grounding force in my life. Never have I sat with someone with such grounded presence, depth, and wisdom; you take the term "holding space" to a whole new level. You lived with us when I was writing this book, and our morning check-ins kept me going on so many levels. You are the steady flame that lights my way, and I am eternally grateful for traveling through these lifetimes with you. Our hearts are connected always. I love you so much. Thank you, babe.

To my son Graham (Grammy) Chalfant: You entered this world and changed the course of my life. I had never experienced such deep and profound love until I met you. You started me on my journey of the heart. This led me to deepen my understanding of emotions and the body. This book wouldn't be possible without that journey that I started the day I first met you. I love you so much, babe. Thank you for choosing me to be your mom.

To my mother, Nancy Brindisi, and my father, Thomas Brindisi (deceased 2001): You both gave me the experience of unconditional love throughout my life (with the exception of my senior year in high school). ☺ You never gave up on me and loved me like no others. Thank you for being my guides on this planet and for always encouraging me, supporting me, and loving me so deeply. I love you both dearly and always will. Thank you.

To Jennifer Dawn: You have been a practitioner, coach, guide, and friend to me. I am beyond ecstatic that we are together in this lifetime. You were with me every step of the way with not only this book but with my business and my life at large. You have been a constant source of grounded support, encouragement, and celestial wisdom. During the many ups and downs in my life and business while I wrote this book, you reassured me that everything was in divine order and divine time, even when I felt like my life was falling apart. You were my lighthouse guiding me through the dark night of the soul. I am eternally grateful for you. Thank you.

To Kristen Shoates: The words "thank you" feel inadequate when I reflect on our six-year journey together, including the creation of this book. I am profoundly grateful not only for having you as a part of the team but also for the incredible support you provided throughout this process. You understood my vision and played an essential role in bringing it to life. As I've told you countless times, "You know me better than anyone," and your help with this book has been invaluable. Thank you for everything, and I look forward to our next collaboration!

To my friends and soul sisters: Karen Campion, Lucy Caminiti, Claudine Sweeney, Karen Gelstein, Annie Boerner, Ramona Reid, Patti Park, and Meghan Crough. Without a doubt, this is not our first rodeo together. I am so blessed to have you as part of my sisterhood in this lifetime. Your constant support, love, and encouragement are ALWAYS next level. I love you all dearly and words cannot express the amount of love I have for each and every one of you. Thank you, sweet sisters.

To my fur babies, Maya and Sully: Maya (RIP June 2024), you were at my feet for nearly sixteen years, whether I was inside or outside. You were my rock, my anchor. I felt as though part of your life purpose was to absorb my frustrations and overwhelm. Thank you for doing that and being here for every part of this book until the very end, when you decided to pass on and help from the other side. Sully, I think we misnamed you and should have called you "Happy." Anytime I was frustrated or had writer's block, you were always ready for a walk in the woods so I could air out my frustrations and gain clarity. You bring me back to my center and my heart just by looking at you (always with a Frisbee in your mouth) and the swing of your tail. I love you both and am so grateful for your never-ending dedication and love for me. Thank you.

To Source/God/Universe, and to all the spirit guides, ascended masters, angels, elementals, birds, my lake, and trees: What a game this thing called life is. Thank you for guiding me, for listening to my whining, and for celebrating my wins. Thank you for the countless hours of talking during my morning walks through the woods along the lake. You all held me in the most grounded space. You offered me a place to vent, percolate my ideas, and gain clarity. So many downloads led to voice recordings for this book. My morning walks were incredible because of your presence. Sometimes I'd hear laughter, lots of wisdom, and most of all, encouragement. Thank you for never letting me down, always being there, and guiding me every step of the way with this book and in life. I'm looking forward to our next book-writing adventure! Thank you, and I love you all.

Resources

There are countless ways to incorporate the Adult Chair into your life. Let your heart guide you. What feels right for you? Where do you feel drawn?

Visit my website, **theadultchair.com/starthere**, where you will find everything from *The Michelle Chalfant Show* to live events and everything in between.

If you are interested in ongoing monthly support, you can become a member of The Academy of Awakening: **theacademyofawakening.com**.

If you feel the pull to help others and the methods in this book resonated deeply with you, perhaps you'd like to explore becoming a Certified Adult Chair Coach. You can find out more about the next program here: **theadultchair.com/ certification**.

If you'd like to work with someone who is certified in the Adult Chair model, find our coaches here: **theadultchair .com/coaches**.

Resources

If you are interested in courses and free resources, head to **courses.theadultchair.com.**

If you're interested in doing more work to connect with your inner child, visit **theadultchair.com/innerchild.**

If you'd like to go deeper with courses that teach you healthy relationship skills, visit **theadultchair.com/relationships.**

Notes

Chapter 1: The Child Chair

1. Association for Psychological Science, "Can Fetus Sense Mother's Psychological State? Study Suggests Yes," Science-Daily, November 10, 2011, http://www.sciencedaily.com/releases/2011/11/111110142352.htm. The study this article summarizes is Curt A. Sandman, Elysia Poggi Davis, and Laura M. Glynn, "Prescient Human Fetuses Thrive," *Psychological Science* 23, no. 1 (January 2012): 93–100, published online December 14, 2011, https://doi.org/10.1177/0956797611422073.
2. "Brain Architecture," Center on the Developing Child, Harvard University, accessed August 28, 2024, https://developingchild.harvard.edu/science/key-concepts/brain-architecture.

Chapter 5: *Pillar Two:* I Practice Self-Compassion

1. Kristin D. Neff, "The Role of Self-Compassion in Development: A Healthier Way to Relate to Oneself," *Human Development* 52, no. 4 (June 2009): 211–214, https://www.ncbi.nlm.nih.gov/pmc/articles/PMC2790748/#B9.

Chapter 6: *Pillar Three:* I Feel My Emotions

1. Jill Bolte Taylor, PhD, *My Stroke of Insight: A Brain Scientist's Personal Journey* (New York: Viking, 2008).
2. Louise Hay, "Louise Hay on Health," accessed August 28, 2024, https://www.louisehay.com/health/.
3. Louise Hay, "Emotional and Mental Causes of Illness: The List," Heartland Healing Arts, June 19, 2018, https://www.heartlandhealingarts.com/blog/2018/6/19/emotional-and-mental-causes-of-illness-the-list-by-louise-hay.

About the Author

———————— ✍ ————————

MICHELLE CHALFANT, MS, LPC, is a renowned therapist, holistic life coach, and transformational leader dedicated to awakening consciousness and empowering individuals to live their best lives. With a rich background in mental health, spirituality, and personal development, Chalfant combines her expertise to offer a comprehensive approach to healing and growth.

Chalfant developed the Adult Chair model, a revolutionary framework where simple psychology meets grounded spirituality. This model guides individuals through the process of understanding who we are and how we got this way. The five pillars guide us into our Adult Chair, the healthiest version of ourselves. It has transformed countless lives, providing practical tools for emotional well-being and personal empowerment.

In addition to her coaching and therapeutic work, Chalfant hosts *The Michelle Chalfant Show,* a popular podcast with over ten million downloads. The podcast delves into a wide range of topics related to personal growth, emotional health, and spiritual development, offering listeners valuable insights and actionable advice. Through her engaging episodes, Chalfant helps people navigate life's challenges and discover their true potential.

As the founder of the Adult Chair Coaching Certification Program, Chalfant has trained and mentored a new generation of coaches who are spreading her impactful methods worldwide. Her commitment to holistic healing is evident through her live events, retreats, and online courses, which offer immersive experiences designed to facilitate deep transformation.

Chalfant's work is a beautiful fusion of spirituality and psychology, making complex concepts accessible and practical. Her warm and relatable approach has made her a beloved figure in the personal development community. She passionately believes in the potential for every person to awaken to their true selves and create a life filled with purpose and joy.

Chalfant resides on a serene lake just north of Charlotte, North Carolina, which she lovingly calls her writing sanctuary and a haven for recharging when she's not traveling to share *The Adult Chair*. She shares her home with her husband and their beloved dogs. Her two grown sons, who are her pride and joy, visit often.

For more information about Michelle Chalfant's offerings, including her podcast, transformative events, courses, and coaching certification, visit theadultchair.com.

Facebook: @TheMichelleChalfant
Instagram: @TheMichelleChalfant
YouTube: @MichelleChalfant